WHEN A DOCTOR FALLS ILL

True Stories and Concepts for the Bad Times

Ugbede Victor Ahiaba

When a Doctor Falls Ill

Dedications

Susan (wife), Peniel(son), Janiel(daughter) and to all the women that raised me –Rose Uchia (mother), Sarah (aunt) and Grandma Amina (paternal, ceteris paribus).

Acknowledgment

Engr. Prof T.K. Philips & Mrs. Rita I. Anurioha for taking their time to read the draft many years ago. A posthumous acknowledgement to Mr. Noah Abuh (may his soul rest in peace), for his numerous calls and messages, to encourage me not to give up on anything.

CONTENTS GUIDE

Chapter One 8
THE BIG PICTURE 8
CHAPTER RECAP 20

Chapter Two 28
YOUR LIFE CAN BE RUINED BY YOUR ENVIRONMENT 28
CHAPTER RECAP 37

Chapter Three 39
DESTINY OR DECISION? 39
CHAPTER RECAP 49

Chapter Four 51
THOUGHTS VS REALITY 51
CHAPTER RECAP 54

Chapter Five 55
GRAVITY VS FAITH 55
CHAPTER RECAP 61

Chapter Six 62
CAUSE AND EFFECT 62
CHAPTER RECAP 67

Chapter Seven 68
THE UNIVERSAL LAW OF REPRODUCTION 68
CHAPTER RECAP 73

Chapter Eight 75
FIRST IMPRESSION 75

CHAPTER RECAP 80
Chapter Nine 81
　　　THE MINDS OF THE GODS 81
　　　CHAPTER RECAPS 90
Chapter Ten 91
　　　GIVING 91
　　　CHAPTER RECAP 97
Chapter Eleven 99
　　　WILLS 99
　　　CHAPTER RECAP 106
Chapter Twelve 108
　　　SUCCESS 108
　　　CHAPTER RECAP 132
Chapter Thirteen 137
　　　WHEN MAN IS TO BLAME 137
　　　CHAPTER RECAPS 150
Chapter Fourteen 152
　　　WHEN GOD IS TO BLAME 152
　　　CHAPTER RECAPS 166
Chapter Fifteen 167
　　　THE WAY FORWARD 167
　　　CHAPTER RECAPS 178
Chapter Sixteen 180
　　　STRATEGIZE WITH PARTNERSHIP 180

Chapter Seventeen 184
TAKE THE RISK..184
Chapter Eighteen 193
BE USEFUL..193

Chapter One
THE BIG PICTURE

About 2009 after my graduation from the university, my father had called me for some unsolicited chats. He began by saying there were three most important dates in the life of every man: the dates of birth, of marriage and of death.

I had started wondering where the conversation was headed, but soon realized he was angry at me for going to my part-time job at a nearby computer centre and then forgetting to load up electricity metres at the metering office, 10 km away. I did not forget actually; I went there late!

It was on a Saturday, and the metering office closed early on Saturdays, and I did not know. I was at work but planned to arrive at the metering office before the normal closing time of 5PM. I arrived to meet closed doors: they had closed at 2PM. In those days, you must travel to the electricity supplier's office to be able to top up, unlike now that you can do this and more on phone or computer.

What we had would not run out before Monday, "I will load it up first thing on Monday, sir," I apologetically replied. That reply did not go down well. In a twinkle, I was bleeding from the top of my right eye. He had hit my face with something I can't remember till date.

Whether he read off the "three most important dates in the life of every man" phrase from a book or conceived it himself, I could not connect it to my failing to load up an electricity metre. All I can recall now is that at my birth, he was absent. He had disowned the pregnancy that led to my birth. He was also absent during my wedding ceremony in 2012. He refused to be a part of it. Two down, one more to go – the death date, and he must be absent too, right? Our relationship has been really bad.

It was in September 1995 that I understood, in clear terms, the story about my life, and that of my mother. I was 13 years old when a woman in my mother's village walked up to me and said these words:

"He will come for you. His first child from his wife is a girl; he will come for you".

I wanted to say something. Like asking her who she was talking about, but I could not say a word. I just stood there like someone that had been hypnotized.

Then she ran her fingers through my hair, hugged me, patted me on the back, squatted right before me and then looked straight into my eyes and said,

"May God favour you; your mother will find herself again through you".

She then greeted some women that were returning from a nearby stream carrying bowls of water on their heads.

I stood there with many questions in my head. Who is the "he" that will come for me? Why should I celebrate because the person she was talking about just had a baby girl from his wife? How could my mother's happiness be something to be found in me?

And sometimes in the future, when I may have received "God's favour"?

I was completely lost in thought. I always do.

About this time, I had lived with many "paternal relatives" assuming everything about my paternity was correct. It dawns on me soon after, that at age 13, I had no clear memorable picture of what my father looked like, where he was and what I meant to him. Could I have seen him and not know him? I had no idea. No one said anything but I knew there was something about me, about my mother and the man between us.

The only time I got a hint was when I had an issue with an older boy in a village called Ulaja, located in the eastern part of Kogi State, Nigeria. It was not unusual for me to challenge certain norms at that time. For example, older people could literally slice kids' football into two for mistakenly kicking it to where elders are seated. I would challenge issues like this one way or another. I had even nurtured the idea of deflating their bicycle tyres as some kind of revenge. I didn't.

So, I had this issue with an older boy, and I was really upset and wanted the fight between us to continue. My grandma came into the picture, and after failing to persuade me to give up the fight, she said these words:

"I am not sure my son is your father at all. No one in my bloodline is this adamant!"

From this moment, I literally transformed from being a free, spirited boy, to a thinker. Rather than questioning my surroundings, I began to question myself and everything between me and the world.

When I was 7 years old, my aunt, Ele, asked me to go to the only primary school in the village to start school. Normally, parents or someone older would assist in the enrolment process. She did not follow me there; I think she did not know how the process worked. In those days, male kids had a better chance of attending school than females. I never saw her go to school at any time.

She had given me some bright coloured shirts that looked like a school uniform from elsewhere and set me on my way. For some reason, she said the school environment would be the right place for me.

So, I walked myself to school for the very first time.

About this time, most children would have to be about ten years before they are allowed into Primary One. There were no nursery schools. In fact, the children may have to be able to wrap their right hand round the back of their necks and be able to see their own fingers through the left-hand side of their faces before they are allowed into Primary 1. It was the strangest test ever. Of course, many people then had no recorded date of birth, so this was used as a test of age.

When the then Headmaster asked for my name and surname, I did not know my surname. I gave my grandmother's name instead, but he said he would not register me with a female name, and in my case, it was a combination of names, starting with *mama*".

Or *Iye* (mother of), followed by one of the children of the mother being referred to. In this community, young people do not call older people by their given names, especially when the older people have children. "My name is Ugbede, and my surname is 'Iye Rhoda (Mama Rhoda)'", I said in Igala dialect.

It did not go down well.

I went back home to ask my grandmother who provided the correct name. My father was absent.

I had to repeat the name she gave me every second as I ran back to the headmaster.

At another time, I was living with my aunt, *Iye Ele*. One of the things I observed was that her husband was always threatening her, telling her to take the "bastard" away from his house. I did not even know what being a bastard meant at that point. But she often insists in her defence that her "brother" was responsible for the child.

Incidentally, this my aunt had only daughters, three of them. But the husband had another wife, with sons and daughters. I could add one and two together and concluded that my aunt was trying to rescue me to become her male child. She may not be too sure if the brother was responsible for the pregnancy that led to my birth. Could she had fought for me because she needed a male child? I do not know.

Maybe not!

My father had rejected me as his child long before I was even born, and that alone was my major predicament till date. It simply hurts.

Back to my encounter with the woman earlier in September 1995 when a female child had been born to my father, in some part of African cultures, if a man has no son, he is considered childless, sort of. The women are always to blame for having only female children. To continue a man's "family name", he must have a son, through whom the family name would be preserved. So, my father just had a daughter from his wife, which the woman considered a good omen for me, a second chance to have my father come for me or accept me.

I forgot to even add that the woman even wished my father would only have daughters!

Oh yes! She wanted me to be accepted and loved at all costs.

I must say at this point that having female or male children makes no difference at all.

Every child matters.

Every child is special.

No child should be valued less or more solely because of the gender they carry. Or how they were born. The important thing is that a child (someone) has been born.

The key thing about my story is that I was born out of wedlock, and my mother is 13 years older than myself!

But what really happened?

Being born outside wedlock, in most cultures in Nigeria and Africa, has some form of stigmatization for those involved: father, mother, the offspring, and even the extended families of both families! The mother, and her family bear the stigma more.

It connotes irresponsibility.

For me, it was a long walk figuring out what was going on in my life then. Many had blamed my mother for having a child at a noticeably immature age. The case was opposite for me: I was blaming the man who got her pregnant.

Sometimes, you begin to value certain things by coincidence. When a friend sent me a small video clip about a woman in a delivery theatre, it changed my perspective about mothers and women. Massively.

It was one afternoon, my phone had just beeped. It was a video clip. When I pressed the Play button, the video began with a woman in birth labour. She was being told repeatedly by the nurses to "push harder!" She pushed harder until the baby's head started to show up, then the rest of its body, with the doctors assisting, by pulling the baby's body out gently.

In the video, nurses were shown moving around the labour room, the camera focused on the woman's face, to clearly show the anguish of childbearing. The last part of the video showed blood on the floor, then a crying beautiful baby, and it ended.

I waited a few seconds, pondering on it, and then punched on the "play" button again. And again.

I began to appreciate how my about 13-year-old mum pushed me out of her body onto some broad cocoyam leaves (I was told) at the back of her father's house. I could imagine the freedom she must have felt after those humiliating months, carrying an unsolicited pregnancy for a man who was nowhere around.

My mother suffered humiliations because she had brought disgrace to her family. I imagined how she managed the situation. I imagined many things. In the early 80s, there was no telephone, so, she couldn't have called my father living in the city, to inform him of the pregnancy.

Some older ladies tried to help her get rid of the pregnancy using herbs. It did not work. I survived.

While thinking of the circumstances, a new dimension of thought crawled through my mind. The thoughts were full of questions on just one thing: Destiny.

Was my mother "destined" to begin her life this way? Who had authored her life this way?

How about me? Was I destined to be born like that too? What gave my teenage mum the ability or audacity to have a child, even when she was not nearly ready to become a mother?

Is it destiny that determines people's decisions, or it is their decisions that determine their destiny? Who gives children (I was told in church that children are gifts from God?). Does it mean God gave a teenager, a baby? What could God be thinking?

Why are some babies born with severe complications anyway?

Why do good people experience evil sometimes, and evil people sometimes experience some good things in life? Challenges of life do not seem targeted only at some groups of religious unbelievers. The pleasures of life do not locate only some religious extremists too. What is going on?

Do miracles happen outside religious houses? Of course, yes!

But why?

CHAPTER RECAP

Here is my conclusion on this: there are certainties that some things would happen no matter what or who is involved. We are all subject to these certainties equally.

But how do we know these certainties? They are rooted in three cores:

- ✓ The Natural or Universal Laws
- ✓ Decision
- ✓ The environment

We have heard many times that "no one can cheat nature." Yes, it is because no one can. While we may think we have cheated nature sometimes, it usually fights back, overruling whatever we felt we got away with.

The natural laws are generous. The laws answer anyone that meets the stipulated or required conditions. Nature guarantees this fact.

And the natural laws are the reason my mother, a teenager, could get pregnant. You heard that right, uh?

She met the requirement for pregnancy.

Natural laws are the reasons why the sun still gives its light to everyone, irrespective of religious background or whatever, good or bad.

We live, grow, and die because nature has determined it so.

Even miracles cannot take place without these fundamental laws in place. For a woman to be pregnant, for instance, she must have to mate with a man at the very right period. Right?

Nature is also generally unfair – because it is too generous! It creates a chain effect. If a married man chooses to go after prostitutes for instance, he may get infected with sexually transmitted disease. The faithful wife at home would become a beneficiary of his adventures.

The opposite scenario produces the same effect.

This leads us to the second core:

Decision!

Next to Universal or natural laws is the decision to do certain things or not. A decision is a powerful force. So powerful that it has consequences every time it is actioned or *not actioned*. If you actioned a business idea, it may fail. It may also succeed. Right? Okay. What if you do not act on a business idea? Well, you are worse than those who actioned their ideas and failed! Whatever you do or do not do, is still a decision that has been made (even by not doing anything at all).

What happens if we decide to place the right seed in the right soil at the right time? Boom! The first core kicks in. Nature will bring a harvest consequently. What happens if we put a good seed on a rock in suitable weather? Scarcity ensues. There will be no harvest because the terms and conditions for the seed to grow and produce, had not been met.

The *environment* is the third core. Like the decision to drop the right seed in the proper soil (environment), if you associate with the wise, you will have wisdom. If you associate with the rich, you have more chances of becoming rich. If you associate with fools, you can become foolish.

The bottom line is that the environment you associate with can determine who you *will* become.

If you associate with thieves, you will become a thief. It does not matter if you ever stole something or not, if your friends keep stealing, and the association is maintained, you are a thief and the consequences that will befall them, could equally come to you.

These three cores are always behind a doctor falling ill!

So, here we are.

Technically, you got what you got because nature answers anyone who meets its terms and conditions; *that's universal or natural laws.* Your current position is a product of past choices; *that is the consequence of a decision.* Activities or implications of one-person's lifestyle do not often affect the person in question alone, but it could affect others around as well; *that is the environment.*

Throughout this book, I will be referencing the life experiences of people, including myself, being a typical out-of-wedlock child, who fought against all odds to find my own place. I can relate what it means to be there.

By the foundation laid by someone else, I was bricking for destruction. The atmosphere was always toxic. Hope was at a far distance. However, I had a focus.

Everyone needs focus, motivation, and passion for self-determination. Yes! Everyone born of a woman has a purpose in life. The quest is to discover that purpose. Those purposes would be manifested by the three cores mentioned earlier – *the natural/universal laws, decisions, and the environment.*

Listen, ladies and gentlemen, while it is true that everyone has a purpose in life, the onus is on you to find your place. You should discover your purpose first, then meet the terms and conditions to actualize it.

Of course, there will be distractions – sometimes, from birth, as in my case. However, learn to put the distractions where they belong, and use them for your purpose – as stepping-stones to your risings- then dump them. Let the end of every matter be better than the beginning.

You need to build up inspirational philosophies for yourself sometimes because your values are shaped by your own personal beliefs. Even the most optimistic person needs motivation and support.

The purpose of this book is to help someone scale through certain hurdles, especially those who have been traumatized by the nature of their birth, environment, or parent's decision. Of course, anyone could find something useful from it too. Find out why that "thing" happened to you and not someone else. The moment you realize the thing or person that may be holding you down from seeing the big picture, or dreaming big dreams, make sure you respond by making appropriate changes immediately. I learnt this truth a little late.

Chapter Two
YOUR LIFE CAN BE RUINED BY YOUR ENVIRONMENT

"The Nurse is dying!" a distant relative I went to visit had exclaimed as she narrated the story of a nurse who was overseeing her community's clinic. Though she was a professional nurse, the villagers often called her a doctor, because she was technically the nurse and the doctor, as there was no doctor in the clinic.

"How can a doctor be sick"? I reasoned. My fragile young brain could not understand it. "A doctor is sick and dying!" I also exclaimed. I was about 7 years old.

When a doctor falls ill, and he/she is unable to get a cure, the question that every one of us would ask is:

You treat others to get well again, but yourself, you cannot?

It is a tricky question to answer. Fear is created if your own invention or training turns out to take your own life. Ask anyone that has become a victim of his or her own profession or circumstance. They will struggle to defend themselves.

Now, if you have been first before and somehow, you become the last, you would understand what I mean. When you see evil prevailing over good, you would feel me too.

Most disheartening are situations where someone's errors (like a pilot's error) or sins do not only affect them alone but everyone around them, leaving many people with the same question; *why*?

Why should some people suffer for things they know nothing about? Why should someone else commit a crime and another person innocently go to jail? The fastest in a race, or the swift, does not win a competition all the time, why? In fact, there are more questions than the available answers in the world today.

To take it all in as simply as possible, some people would say, "such is life."

My school mate, *Gideon* (pseudonym), struggled through life up to 400 Level in the university and then died to a strange disease he inherited from his parents.

Another school mate called *John* (pseudonym), was a devoted Christian, a prayer warrior. John was experiencing severe heat around the left side of his head, so bad that he could hardly read his books. He prayed like no other but in pain. In John's case, the result of his hurting head was his bad academic performance, which eventually left him behind in school while the rest had graduated. He appeared as the "friend" of God, but he was having a problem that doctors had fought and lost over (according to him). Yet, the Creator of the universe, including John's hurting head, could not get him a solution. The last time I spoke with John, he had lost interest in education and, everything else, including God!

If virginity is anything to be proud of, either by God or by humanity, then the story of *Linda* (pseudonym) should leave you speechless. Linda got married as a virgin, but the rich man who married her did so because he heard that if someone with human immunodeficiency virus (HIV) had sexual intercourse with a virgin, the infection would be cleared from the carrier. Linda got married for love or whatever, the man he married was looking for a cure. That was how Linda became an HIV infected widow.

Not all that glitters is gold, every one of us must understand that only we can make our lives beautiful here on earth. Look, look again, before you leap.

If *Caleb* (pseudonym) had known that stopping by the roadside to help a pregnant woman was a trap by armed robbers, he would have ran-off for his dear life. He wanted to help someone in need, but he was robbed of his valuables.

Many situations are so heartbreaking that it is pointless listing more than necessary.

The children of Israel came across several issues like these years ago, and they said:

"...the way of the Lord is not equal" (Ezekiel 18 vs., 25, 29 KJV)

The old Prophet Jeremiah had once wondered over this matter, and he observed that:

"For among my people are found wicked men: they lay wait as he that sets snares; they set a trap, they catch men. As a cage is full of birds, so are their houses full of deceit: therefore, they become great and waxed rich. They are waxen fat, they shine yes, they overpass the deeds of the wicked: they judge not the cause, the cause of the fatherless, yet they prosper; and the right of the needy do they, not judge." (Jeremiah 5:28 KJV).

The Prophet made that contention thousands of years ago, and it is the same way things are still happening today. It could mean that there are indeed some laws governing these occurrences. This is the gap this book would fill, and I hope it provides you support to overcome whatever you may be going through right now.

When a Doctor Falls Ill

Back to the Nurse story earlier, she resided by the market square across the major road that linked the village and the nearby town. She was the one in charge of the clinic named after the community. As I got to know years later, due to shortage of medical doctors, this young, beautiful, and intelligent woman turned out to be the head of the clinic where she was the only staff!

Doctors do not want to stay in the village for obvious reasons.

In case of any emergency in the night hours, the clinic had one bush lamp that helps illuminate some portion of the "Waiting Room:" - the only room that serves every purpose.

The Nurse, despite these challenges, remained in the village, caring for the people. Virtually everything she needed to do her job was in short supply. Even the syringes for injections were very inadequate. Sometimes, one needle could be used for several patients a day. In some cases, it left some children paralyzed for life.

The burden was much.

The rural people reciprocated her care and passion with some of their harvests from the farm: yams, corn, plantain, banana of various species, you name them. Everyone worked hard to have something to give to the Nurse as appreciation for serving them.

She was the most famous person in the entire village. Perhaps, only a few people have not visited her for one health problem or another.

However, one day, she took ill. The news of her illness spread so quickly like wildfire. The Nurse was dying slowly, of a complicated infection.

A week after, Nurse Bello was gone. She died!

She wanted to live, every person in that village needed her, the entire community went wild with series of cries and questions from every angle, and for every person that stepped into the Nurse's house the day of her death, the only question on their lips was one.

"She treated all of us to get well again, why couldn't she do the same to herself"?

This was not mockery, but a form of trepidation that the well-respected Nurse was ill, and she could not find herself a cure.

The point here is that anytime anything goes wrong with someone who happens to be an expert in a specific field, a series of questions would be asked. To this extent, it is not out of place to ask a doctor why he/she could not get cured. Similarly, if an engineer's design fails in any way, people would ask questions. Even if you are a roofer and the rainstorm blows away your roof, people would ask questions about why it happened to you and not the neighbours who are not in the roofing business. When men become victims of what they preach, what becomes of their message?

According to a Scottish philosopher, Thomas Reid, *"laws of nature are the rules to which the effects are produced. But there must be a cause which operates according to these rules. The rules of navigation never navigated a ship, and the rules of architecture never built a house."*

In other words, nothing happens unless the environment (someone or something), makes it happen.

When I was in the university, there was a Sport-viewing Centre close to the campus where all kinds of people go to watch live football matches. Even criminals go there too! Of course, the Sport viewing Centre was on police watchlist. The police often raided this location during big football matches. I was told of someone that came to watch football but was arrested along with some known thieves who also happened to be there watching a game. He spent about 2 years in custody - awaiting trial. Why? He was in the wrong environment.

When a Doctor Falls Ill

The people you associate with matters!

They can become your environment, and when you are caught up with them, there are consequences. Your environment could be your friends, it could be your parents' house too. It could be your current place of work or the house you live in. If you are not seeing the progress you expected, it may be right you consider a change.

Letting a house that does not allow occupants to own cars could be a mental limitation. Change residence. If you can no longer dream big dreams in a place, change your location. If a country, city, or town is draining you, consider a change too.

CHAPTER RECAP
Common sense can elevate a common person, lift a person from the dunghill and place him/her in the limelight of glory where he/she can dine and wine with kings and queens. Listen to the wisdom of Bob Marley (1945 - 1981), a Jamaican musician, singer, and songwriter, in his Uprising, "Redemption Song",

that says *Emancipate yourselves from mental slavery, none but only you can free your mind.*

Make changes that change you for good! Your life can be ruined by your environment.

Chapter Three
DESTINY OR DECISION?

If there is at least one reason for anything that has ever happened under the sun, then, an explanation can be given to everyone's life on the issue of destiny and decision.

By simple definition, destiny connotes something that must happen in the future, it cannot be tainted neither can it be avoided. On the other hand, decisions are choices or judgment that you make after a thought.

This reminds me of a Sunday School teaching in a local church many years ago. The teacher had told us that we would be judged according to our individual destinies. It kept me wondering for a long time because I now understand that destiny cannot be changed. Some said it could only delay, but it cannot be denied or tainted. Even delays in the fulfilment of a destiny should be counted as part of the destiny, right? Okay. It means that before our births, our destinies had been written or created. It implies that harlotry had been written for the harlots, stealing for thieves, killing for murderers, and president for our president.

I do not agree with this school of thought because it does not hold true.

Too many people have relied so much on destiny to the point that, if they have a problem with their home, they will say it is in their destiny. If they were involved in an accident, they would say it is in their destiny. If they fail a particular course in school, they will say it is in their destiny. Even when people lose a loved one in death, they would say it is in their destiny.

A thousand and one things could have caused any of these scenarios, but destiny is not one of them.

That I was born out of wedlock is not in my destiny. It was someone's decision. And I realized that everyone's choices consummate into destiny. It is only on this foundation that our actions can be justified or punished. We are where we are today because of the decisions we made in time past.

When a Doctor Falls Ill

Tomorrow, we will be somewhere because of the choices of today and that of yesterday combined.

So, when my mother told me that it was in her *destiny* to be where she is today, lacking, and unsatisfied with her life, I did not agree. Her present situation is a direct result of her *decision* (voluntary or forced) and the choice of others around her.

She became a mother at an early age because of someone's decision. And perhaps, hers too.

However, as the former President of the United States, Barrack Obama once said, we *can reclaim our dreams*. This is all we can do right now. It is no time to blame anybody, it is time to reclaim your dreams, to turn the table around and find your place.

It is no time to regret either, it is time to recover your dreams. This is what you should be doing right now. Begin to take steps. Reclaim the lost paths.

A good friend of mine, whom I would prefer to call Akuma (pseudonym), can be a living testimony of how decisions shape destinies. Now in his thirties, he told me he just grew up to find himself in a large family with poor parents. Both his primary and college schools were in the commercial city of Lagos, Nigeria, where he learned the Catholic faith and discipline. As a teen, he had some excellent qualities and skills: active, smart, a great footballer, outstanding in technical drawing, especially those related to buildings.

However, he had an antagonistic and pessimistic friend who never believed in him. He never thought Akuma's dream of being an Architect was possible. He had good reasons to doubt Akuma's vision: Akuma had poor parents, and studying Architecture was an expensive venture.

That was in the late '90s.

Six years after secondary school, Akuma was yet to secure admission to any higher institution. Reason: financial obscurity. By this time, "everything" according to him, "was pointing nowhere" as the future was vague and lacked any definite point desirable.

It seemed to him he was in the wilderness, and those six years were indeed wasted. In the six years period, he had worked in several places – including catering, printing press, and construction sites.

He had sold palm oil in an open market for four years, out of those six years!

With all these "work experiences", his life was heading nowhere in particular.

"Is this how I will become a respected human being?" he would ask himself rhetorically. He knew the answer. It was a no.

However, one day, he came across a small pamphlet titled, "Discover your Destiny," in which he learned that every man should have at least a five-year plan. So, he decided to have his own projects. One of it was to get into a university.

After battling with what he would study in school since his good friend was not even encouraging him for the architectural course, he prayed for a sign – just something that could point him in a direction. Somehow, someone unexpectedly gifted him an old, unwanted architecture book! This gift re-ignited his passion for his dream course. He felt he had been noticed by God. He asked for a sign, a gift was given to him.

Akuma was also a talented artist. He discovered this the day an Artist came around his palm oil shop looking for something. The artist met Akuma reading a book, and then asked to know what he was reading. A conversation ensued that led to the Artist knowing that he was studying to become an Architect! He was not really convinced Akuma could become an Architect since he felt Akuma could not make drawings.

He even told him he does not look like someone that would see the four walls of a university. In the process of this conversation, a contest ensued. The

Artist told him to sketch on paper, a woman walking into her office in two minutes.

Akuma won the challenge.

The surprised Artist then engaged him in his creative work – making Greeting Cards and Banners.

One day, Akuma brought an old magazine that had an ancient Benin masquerade in it. His Artist boss reproduced it, which he later sold at a substantial amount - one of his best sales at the time. When Akuma got to know of this development, he requested for his share since he was the one that brought the old magazine.

He received a peanut he asked for. It was just a soft drink.

Akuma was sad for asking for so little. However, he leaned to demand the best value on anything, from that moment onward. He was angry at his own foolishness.

With this anger, he pursued the admission process more rigorously and secured it.

At this point, he had decided to make his wishes happen.

According to Robert Schuler, the most important lesson for anyone facing risks in their desire to succeed is to *focus on the risks that are your sole responsibility.*

In other words, for destiny to manifest, everyone has a part to play. Play your part first. Leave the rest to God.

Akuma had not read Schuler's book titled *Don't throw away tomorrow* at this point. Still, he was unconsciously applying the principle of "do your part first."

Today, as I write these lines, Akuma is a renowned Architect! He now lives in what used to be a "future" or dreams.

Many people want to identify with him.

What about Akuma's siblings; they are not as "lucky" as Akuma. I decided to put that word *lucky* in quotes because it was not luck that brought Akuma this far. Instead, it was Akuma's will. He simply turned around his way off the *wilderness*, to paradise instead.

What about Akuma's friend who told him that his dream of attending a higher institution to become an Architect was a misapprehension? Well, it took Akuma just a phone call, to inform him years after, that he had become an Architect.

Akuma overcame his fears, financial obscurity, challenges, and the parent's inability to contribute meaningfully. He succeeded against all the odds with just one weapon: decision to win.

Opportunities abound. However, some readiness is required on the part of the beneficiary.

The moment you meet the conditions attached to every occasion, something positive must happen.

That is, the results of obedience become so undisputable. It does not matter who you are. It does not matter where you come from. It does not matter how you were born. What matters is your ability to meet the terms and conditions attached.

So, is it destiny that defines decisions or it is decisions that determine the future? The answer is now apparent, I am sure. If Akuma had chosen to play safe and continue selling his palm oil, he would not have come this far in architectural design business. He probably wouldn't have ended up a great palm oil seller.

He could have blamed his parents and say, "my parents have no money to send me to school." Good argument, but it would not have brought him this far. It is a fact.

Can you see now that it is man's decisions that create his life and destiny rather than destiny creating decisions?

Your way or path determines your end. Decisions always come before action, and every man's choice is his destiny.

CHAPTER RECAP

If you observed carefully on the Dedication Page, I mentioned *to all the women who raised me.* The reason is personal. I am alive here authoring this book because of women. My 13-year-old mother, against all the odds, refused to abort me. She handed me over to my aunt, who accepted me with all the consequences.

Following several persecutions from her husband, she handed me over to my *paternal* grandmother. I had lived with other people temporarily too, but my final home was with my grandmother.

My grandmother defined who I am today.

She frowns at anything that causes pain to people or even *things*! For instance, you cannot place a stool on a broom and sit on it; she would say something like, "if the broom is not sweeping, then let it rest!".

She detests those who cheat people of their rightful possessions.

These are colours of her inward self, and I admire her life a lot. She built my personality.

While racing towards the goal, do not forget the role of strangers and relatives. As I mentioned earlier, even the most optimistic person needs motivation. Respect people, take cautions where needed, and keep focus on your goal. Eventually, your preparation and opportunity will meet.

Chapter Four
THOUGHTS VS REALITY

People's thoughts (both conscious and unconscious) dictate the reality of their lives, whether they are aware of it or not. What you constantly focus upon will manifest, whether you want it or not. If you've control over your thoughts, you will have control over your reality. If you are a lively person, you will attract lively people. Likes give birth to likes. If you think success, success will come if you work or take actions towards it.

As a man thinks in his heart, so is he; says the Holy Book. The people who have succeeded or who are succeeding are the people who have seen or imagined those successes in their minds. What makes their case different is that they do not only imagine/think, but they also work or take actions towards their imaginations.

You cannot get a result by only praying. Prayers are effective when you back them up with work. Prayers are supposed to be motivations.

No man plants yam and reaps cocoyam or maize. It is what you put in the soil that will grow. God guarantees everyone this. The mind is like the soil. If you fertilize your soil with the right elements needed by your crops, they will grow to bear good fruits and vegetables for you. If on the other hand you choose not to fertilize the soil, what the soil can offer your plants, that is what you will reap. Same goes with your thought.

Work in line with what you are imagining and praying for, eventually, you will see results.

Biblically, it is recorded that *God can do far above your thoughts…* what that means is that you can always go further than your thoughts and works can take you. You are tougher than you think you are when the place of action or work is not neglected.

In the view of the Law of Attraction you simply attract into your life whatever you think about. Your dominant thoughts will find a way to manifest. Many people may find this "attraction" problematic when you look at the law in a literal or objective way. By objective reality, I mean imagining a thing and having it as imagined without a single contribution or action by the person who needs the thing. This will yield practically nothing. You cannot make a car run without fuel or some form of stored energy, just because you imagined it. There cannot be smoke without some element of fire. When a lion feeds, an animal must die in the process. You understand what I mean, right?

What happens when people put out conflicting intentions, like two people intending to get the same promotion when only one position is available? The one who worked for the promotion, and having other form of edge, will get it, all things being equal. The edge could be anything. It could be a relationship built outside of office hours. It could be the flexibility exhibited in workplaces in the past. It could be grace of God at work!

Finally, until you make the unconscious conscious, it will direct your life and you will confuse it for destiny.

This is to say that words upon words without action in the right direction will result in wrong output or nothing at all. In fact, just as faith without work is dead, the same way your thoughts will remain if you do nothing about it to make it real.

It is your decisions that determine your destiny, not the other way round.

CHAPTER RECAP
Robert Green, the author of *The Art of Seduction*, said this: "Use the positive side of [your] emotional osmosis to [your] advantage."

Chapter Five
GRAVITY VS FAITH

Scientifically, gravitation plays a crucial role in most processes on the earth. The gravitational pull of the planet on all objects holds the objects to the surface of the earth. Without it, the spin of the earth would send them floating off into space. It means that without the force of gravity, if you throw an object, the object will remain as you have thrown it never to fall or go sway. A drop of saliva from your mouth will be floating around your mouth, with nothing to pull it down to the ground. Gravity plays a key role in ocean tides and weather changes too.

No man can deny the relevance of this law to life and existence ever since Sir Isaac Newton discovered it when an apple fruit fell on his head while taking a rest under an apple tree.

He asked (paraphrased), "why did that apple fell down and not remained at the stalk"? That singular question created a new vista in science and engineering. We have built flying objects taking into consideration the gravitational force.

How does gravitation relate to the various occurrences of our life's situations? What are its implications?

First, imagine the gravitational force on all objects that keeps them in place to be equal to the force of faith. With faith in place, the next requirement for manifestation of your thoughts lies in the work that you do along with the magnitude of your faith. We have degrees of faith just as the gravitational pull-on objects differs, depending on the location of the object relative to the centre of the force of gravity. Faith connotes working right with hope to achieve a target. It is a "foolish" force that can make an unimaginable impact.

Like gravity, faith is a part our lives. You need to have faith on your spouse to keep the home front at peace and harmony. You need to have faith on people at work and places. You need to have faith in God before he can become a source of hope, inspirations and strength for your body, soul, and mind. You need faith in yourself too. Every area of your life needs this faith.

Therefore, if any man thinks he can disobey this law because he is a man of God, a teacher, a pastor, an engineer etc, let him test the law by jumping from an extremely high point to the ground or floor. Believe me, faith will not respond, and the result will be disaster! The angels will not bear you up as you fall, because it is a natural universal law that must never be taken for granted or be put to test.

Faith works in line with the law and never against it.

What that statement means is that, if you say you have faith, and you are not working accordingly, in line with your faith, nothing good can come out of it. In other words, you will have no proof of your faith if you have no working principles along with it.

Faith without work is dead. The earth will be a dead place without gravity!

Nothing can grow without the working hard to make it grow.

Work along with your faith. Religion has no place here, to secure or exempt or exclude anyone. You can understand this from nature. The sun gives its light to everyone just as the rain and the soil give their goods to every planter. The day these fail to continue as usual, the day the law of gravity fails on earth, that day must be the end of the world.

Every man to himself, God is for all, said the Americans. And it is quite true. People around the world lay too much emphasis on supernaturalism. These set of people go too spiritual too quickly. They rarely sponsor research work in case it would turn out unsuccessful.

Successful people and countries do not operate like that. They try and try, even in the face of challenges that could render some research works dangerous and unprofitable. They know that a failed research work is a successful work because it would have proven a way that some certain things cannot be done.

The forces of gravity and faith are real and unseen. They are times you must never take gravitational force for granted. They are also times you need not "faith" on things whose solutions are already visible. This is because, faith is not evident on things that are already visible. Prayers should be for tackling impossible things.

CHAPTER RECAP

The smallest seed I have ever known is the mustard seed. Ironically, it is one of the biggest canopy trees in the forest. Out of that small seed, a mighty tree often emerges. As you dream big, have faith in your ability to reach those dreams too.

Chapter Six
CAUSE AND EFFECT

The theory of Cause-and-Effect Analysis answer two key questions: "*Why* did this happen?" and

"What might result from this?"

When you are searching for the reasons why a decision was made or an event occurred, you are looking at causes. When you are trying to predict or understand the consequences, you are looking at effects.

The general purpose of causal analysis is to make sense of the events around us. Understanding cause and effect relationships can help us to encourage positive and discourage negative consequences. Anytime you need to explain why something happened or make a prediction about what might happen, a causal analysis is required.

Every action has an equal but opposite action called reaction. It means that whatever we choose to do has its consequences and rewards; hence, once there is a cause, an effect will follow. It may not follow immediately, but surely, it will follow.

The law of cause and effect is an everyday affair. When you disobey a traffic light for instance, you have initiated a cause. If unlucky, the law catches you or you run into other vehicles, those are the effects, the immediate effects. Other effects may as well follow in the long term of it. One, you may sustain injuries if an accident results. Two, you may be fined by the law resulting in monetary loss. Three, if the whole scene results in death, then, you will not only lose your life, but you have caused your family and your country to lose. According to Heraclitus, a Greek philosopher, *"a hidden connection is stronger than an obvious one."*

You can't run away from these things.

A Scottish philosopher, Mr. Hume in the *Treatise of Human Nature* first propagated this law, and he said:

"The only connection or relation of objects, which can lead us beyond the immediate impressions of our memory and senses, is that of cause and effect. Our reason must be considered as a kind of cause, of which truth is the natural effect."

Hume maintained that we have no other notion of a cause but that it is something prior to the effect, which has been found by experience to be constantly followed by the effect. It follows from this definition that night is the cause of day, and day is the cause of night.

We can at this point conclude that humans are the problem of humankind. All the effects of each man's decisions are each man's destiny.

Now, they are some people who believe so much in the unverifiable theory of *luck* and *ill-luck.* Some are born unlucky, they would say. No such things exist anywhere.

Political positions come with power. To gain such powers, for example, becoming a president of a country, comes with enormous work and planning. It is not by luck. To gain this political power requires you to convince the electorates to vote for you. The poor alternative is painstakingly rigging the election.

Either way is not child's play.

It is not easy to convince someone to see through your thoughts, principles, and philosophies. Neither is it easy to scale through the hurdles of rigging an election.

You must first be prepared in every required area – academically, morally, physically, and ideologically and so on. These are the obvious requirements that can prove you worthy.

Some people will say "luck" can play a role in this but, in my opinion, just as that of Joyce Carol, *there is no such thing as "luck."*

In the view of a French Scientist, Pasteur, *"chance favours only the prepared mind."* A chance is an opportunity. It may come your way, but when you are not prepared physically, academically, ideologically, or other areas, there is no way you can get hold of such opportunities. When you get it, you are either qualified in one area or another.

QUOTABLE QUOTES ON THE LAW OF CAUSE AND EFFECT

Divine blessing comes when opportunity meets preparation - Pastor Ayo Orisejafor: Word of Life Bible Church Warri, Nigeria.

We have no other notion of cause and effect, but that of certain objects, which have always conjoined together, and which in all past instances have always been found inseparable - David Hume (1711 - 1776
- Scottish philosopher and historian in *the Treatise of Human Nature.*

To be a catalyst is the ambition most appropriate for those who see the world as being in constant change, and who, without thinking that they can control it, wish to influence its direction - Theodore

Zeldin (1933 -British historian: *An Intimate History of Humanity.*

Method, therefore, in the study of philosophy, is the shortest way of finding effects by their known causes, or of causes by their known effects - Thomas Hobbes (1588 - 1679 - English philosopher and political thinker: *Elements of Philosophy.*

CHAPTER RECAP

This law admits no hold-up. Its application is universal. There is nothing to gain in believing that they can be an effect without a cause. It will only lead you the path of misery, and you may have to pay for it dearly. Every decision you make, or not make, has consequences.

Chapter Seven
THE UNIVERSAL LAW OF REPRODUCTION

The only process that could continuously keep human race going, as well as that of animals and even plants, is the process of reproduction. Without reproduction, humankind would have long gone into extinction, as would the animals, plants, and other formations. This however is made possible under a law, which from the beginning of time, had given every viable offspring the vigour to reproduce its kind.

This is a particularly important law that has further shown that God has given us freedom to make choices. The Holy Book declared that man should "dominate and replenish" the earth and subdue it. No single portion of the law has changed ever since, even though humanity has revolutionized the process, which now involved using other means to actualize the same goal.

Test-tube babies still have that resemblance to the very personality that fertilized the egg or the personality that owns the fertilized egg from which they are conceived and delivered.

And because it is a Universal Law, it has not reshaped or restructure in any form. If a healthy teenage girl chooses to indulge in sexual activity with a sexually mature male, at the right time of ovulation, with minimum sperm quantity and quality required for fertilization to occur, pregnancy will be inevitable. God will never say, "Oh, she is still a child, she does not know what she is doing, therefore no pregnancy," never! God cannot change the law nor break it against himself.

I believe in miracles, but I do not believe that it is God that gives children, rather, it is the process he had already setup from the beginning of time that does it.

In some rare cases, I mean exceedingly rare cases, God himself is responsible for barrenness, same all the cases would have human errors or manipulations, or interruptions. For example, women are often advised to avoid alcohol when pregnant.

This advised is researched-based. Before that, it was possible that some were drinking alcohol while pregnant. Even when the advice started rolling out, some women may still be drinking alcohol in secrecy. It means that when complications follow the childbirth or the child, we may be tempted to say, "we do not know why", but those involved, like the mothers that drank alcohol while pregnant, would know. And only a few of them would spill the bean.

The problem lies with humankind always. They are millions of processes, hormones, and cells in human body that medical science and technology does not know their full behaviour yet, so it is easy for medical experts to say, "You have no problem." Even if there is, because present technologies cannot detect such problems yet, the verdict would be the same.

It is a law, that is why a teenage girl who is already menstruating, can get pregnant at the slightest opportunity.

When a Doctor Falls Ill

What does this tell you? It is telling you that at any point in time that you meet the conditions for anything in life, your wishes no longer have relevance; the universal law takes over from there.

So, it is not God that says you should have a dozen children when you do not have what it takes to feed them. It is your decision to create the rooms for the children to roll in by meeting the conditions. God initiated the processes, or the mechanisms involved, but since he gave that command of replenishing the earth, everyone becomes a user of that process. The mechanisms respond to anyone who presses the right button at the right time. What do you expect of God when you press too many right buttons at the right time? You are only reaping what you have sowed. Similarly, if you are not able to press any right button at the right time, the process will never respond. The ball is always in man's court.

The other day I ran into a woman with triplets begging for support to care for the children. She was begging with one interesting philosophy and song: *It is God that gave us the children; we believe he knows we can cater for them that is why he gave them to us.* With that, I already had one question running haphazardly in my mind: *why was she begging then?*

As people were passing along the streets and dropping a few pennies in her hand, most of them were lamenting and asking God, why he did not give such children to the rich people in the society. Does God *share* children according to financial capability? Does he even share at all!

And will they ever get an answer from God, after he had set the mechanism in motion that can produce children? No, I do not think so. If the rich people they referred to have no children, it is because they have not met the conditions for children. You cannot plant a seed in a dry ground and expect it to germinate. It would need water, air, and good soil to germinate well.

CHAPTER RECAP

This is a hard law to believe too easily, especially when I mentioned that it is not God that gives children. People I have spoken to on this matter while authoring this book, blamed God, or the devil as the cause of having or not having children.

If we keep saying it is God that gives children and quote the portion of the Bible that says, "all good and perfect gifts are from above," then what becomes of some gifts or issues that are obviously not good? There are babies born with both male and female sex organs. Some were cojoined at birth. What is good in this? Others were blind, deaf. Even some had no functional, vital organs like the heart. Some were still births.

The truth of the matter is that we humans have polluted our bodies and our environment with so many catastrophic materials that leaves us vulnerable to hazards and subsequent defects. The world is facing global environmental challenges today not because the creator of the world has changed some certain factors. The sun is still the sun just as the moon. We are reaping the consequences of our actions and inactions.

Chapter Eight
FIRST IMPRESSION

A friend of mine was preparing for a visit to his in-laws to-be for the very first time and as usual, we were busy putting up the necessary stuffs he would need as "greetings" for them. As we were about to leave, the mother noticed something was not in order in his outfit, so she told him "You must give your *first impression* the required "ingredients," after which, she put in her suggestion to make him look better. And she saw well. My friend, Patrick, did not knit his tie properly and some other things too. The emphasis she laid on "first impression" got me into thinking and I discovered from the popular saying that "the way you dress, is the way you will be addressed" is still talking about "impression."

Creating a positive impression on the minds of people around you are especially important, but that of "first impression" is much more important and impacting than all others combined. Just as it is in the Law of Giving, there are many ways of creating this first impression – a gift, a generous act, a kind favour, an honest admission of wrong or right doing, dressing sense to captivate (though care should be taken not to make it look like a show-off or pride) among other forms.

This is because, when your reputation is established, through a well-planned first impression, it is hard to shake. In the words of Robert Green, "selective honesty is best employed on your first encounter with someone." Why? Because *we are all creatures of habit, and our first impressions last a long time."* And like I said earlier, a well-planned impression gives you room (both now and in the future) to deceive, maneuver and even jilt with ease.

I was walking along a pathway during my university days with a friend when he spotted a man on a motorbike few meters away from our position. Immediately, he spotted the man, he lamented *"that man on that motorbike is wicked!"*

When a Doctor Falls Ill

Why did you say that? I asked. *"Nothing, he is just like that,"* he replied. I knew there was more that led to his conclusion that the said man was a wicked man, but he was not prepared to let it out. I was not interested in knowing what went wrong at that point in time, not until about two weeks later when I ran into the said man in the church. The first thing that hit my mind was my friend's first lamentation about the man, saying, *"this man is wicked!"* and I was already making effort to avoid the man right within me.

It happened that way because the statement about him was the first impression of him created by someone else. Imagine that the said person made such an impression on my mind himself, the impacts would have been much more, and might linger on forever in my mind.

The first impression is an idea, a feeling, or an opinion that you get about somebody, or something based on your first experience with them. It is also an idea, a feeling, or an opinion that somebody gives you about other people, based on what the other people did or did not do.

You are meeting a man for the very first time and he begins to tell you how bad his wife has been to him at home, or how Christ loves the church or how bad the economy is affecting everybody, for an exceedingly long time, you are likely to remember the very first day you met, and you are likely to continue to recall the first issues presented or the impression that they created on the first day.

The law of first impression states that you are technically the personality you impressed on others on your first meeting. In other words, people take you as you take or present yourself, especially on your first meeting. If your dress is the first thing that attracts someone at your first meeting, you will be looked at and rated the way you looked. If you display pride on the first date, then you are likely to be judged for sometimes or even forever as a proud person.

What are the implications of this law to life? There are two implications: Positive and Negative. You can maximize this Universal Law to your advantage or to your ruin. Your first impression can determine your overall reputation. According to Robert Greene, the author of the popular *the 48 laws of power*,

"Reputation is the cornerstone of power. Through reputation alone, you can intimidate and win; once it slips however, you are vulnerable, and will be attacked on all sides...meanwhile, learn to destroy your enemies, by opening holes in their own reputations. Then step aside and let the public opinion hang them."

That is an exceptional thought from a world-renowned writer and mentor, Mr. Greene.

The positive impact of creating a good first impression is enormous. So also, are the negative impacts in the down lane. Everything under the sun is judged first by appearance. What is not seen or easily seen counts for nothing much; it is a cob-out.

Impression, reputation, or appearance, whatever it is you want to call it, know now that it can make your career or mar it out rightly from day one! It can destroy your relationship or chop it off you. It can kill your inner courage if it turns against you. Sometimes, the opportunity to correct your first created impression may never be available again.

CHAPTER RECAP
It is necessary for you to draw from the well of wisdom now. The first impression you should learn to create is that of yourself to yourself! No one can give what he or she does not have. For you to radiate light, you must be light to yourself. Therefore, for any man to be able to impress appropriately, not eye service or showing off, he must genuinely have an internal positive impression of himself.

It is my opinion that we are reflections of who we have inwardly.

Chapter Nine
THE MINDS OF THE gods

Back in the village in those days, we were told a story of some short beings usually referred to as "small gods." We were made to believe that these short creatures have great ideas about what men do. Sometimes, they come to the midst of people from the forest where they live to pick up kids without anyone seeing them. They were considered invisible when they did this. However, they will return to the person after some days, weeks, months and even years.

Such "kidnapped" people would usually turn out to become great bicycle repairers, merchants, soothsayers, successful farmers and so on. As we were told, these beings were invisible, but they lived among men and any man they touched or "adopted" would return with great ideas as they (small gods) had.

I lived with this mindset for long before I discovered later in life that the elders were playing tricks on our minds. There were no such things as small gods – we were brainwashed! As at then, children who have been told this story would have a desire either to be adopted by the small gods or dread them completely. I was among the ones who desired to be touched or adopted, so I always look out for them on my way back and forth the farm, for a touch to become a great man. Not until later in life, I did not know that the elders were only saying those tales for one thing – fun! They were just fine-tuning our minds to make us listen, think deeply and be useful.

What is this mind then?

Well, it is a controversial term. Some people take it to mean the signals being produced by the brain as a direct consequence of the sense organs found in human bodies. With this reasoning, it means that when a man dies, his mind dies as well. But this is not the true case of the matter. When a man dies, his spirit lives on but the body decays away. That spirit that "lives on" carries all the information that the dead person had while alive.

It means that when a man dies, the mind remains but its name would transform to mean "Spirit" or Soul. Whichever term anyone chooses to use, the meaning still connotes a person's inner nature, excluding the body. However, the activities of the inner nature, dictates the direction of motion, action, and behaviour of the living body of man. Some people believe that it is what the body does that dictates the direction of thought, but it is the opposite, because before every action, they must have been a thought to take the action.

The Universe is like a hologram, and we are all part of it. Consciousness is very much a part of the equation. The observer and the observed cannot be separated. From scientific point of view, every man has five sense organs: those responsible for sight, hearing, tasting, perceiving, and feeling. However, there exists the Sixth Sense that can make a man see, hear, taste, smells and feel things that are not within his immediate reach. This is called the *mind*.

It is the most crucial unseen force in man because it controls man's thought and hence, his decisions. If you can have power and control over the activities of your mind, then you've full control of your surroundings and all that goes on in it.

There have been major debates and philosophies on the topic of the mind long before the 17th century, and a lot of people have become so interested in it after the 17th century till date. According to the Microsoft Encyclopedia, there has been a persistent problem - The Mind-Body Problem, which tries to correlate the body and the mind. Do the two have effects on one another?

So far, the issue of the mind is a sensitive issue with lots of contradictions in the views of great thinkers and philosophers. However, the mind is that part of you that enables you to be aware of the things around you, to think and feel. It is the root of what we called the five sense organs of *man*. This part of you is the most sensitive of all your being. It is from the mind you read meaning to everything. It is from it you reason out fault and praises.

From the mind, and the understanding of the mind, a mother would know at once if her child has done something wrong. From the mind you sense when it is favourable to have heart to heart talk with your boss, spouse, or even parents. It is the centre of imagination.

Everyone uses his or her mind to think but all thoughts are not the same. Some channel theirs into condemnation and poverty while others to eternal life and life of fulfilment on earth. Some kill with theirs while others make life out of it. The path you channel your thought depends on your understanding of your status and how your status should be.

Many of us are going through similar situations in life, for instance, but not all of us would end up with the same result. Why? Because, where you channel your problems and how you view those problems determines the outcome you will get. The messengers of evil are aware of the importance of the mind in any individual, so they usually make it the first point of attack.

By consolidating a little fault in something or somebody, like a spouse, the mode of worship in your local church or of a particular person in your mind, they have started winning you over to themselves. A faultfinder would have much opposition. A man of much opposition is a man with many enemies. And a man who sees a lot of people as enemies cannot be innocent.

Those who succeed in life are those who channel their mental energy to the positive and sunny side of life. They fail, but they do not see failure as failure but as a step forward. They imagine a new idea from every event, even from a previously failed idea.

It is often said that *"determination through challenging work is the key to success in life'* but that cannot come-by if your mind is not seeing any success picture to arrive at. Show me a determined man and you would have shown me a visionary man. The level of your determination is proportional to the contents of your mind. For example, a married man who wants the best for his family would work hard to utilize every opportunity to save money for his children's education and future. Such a man can deprive himself of some things to fulfill his plans in his mind for his family. But that cannot be the case of a man who has no such plans and desire for his family or who does not even have or intends to have a family.

Hence, the content of the mind determines how industrious one can be in the quest for a fulfilled life. For example, again, as a student, I know what it means to me to have satisfactory results because it may be one of the factors which would determine my chances tomorrow. Therefore, if at any point in time I discover that I am getting lazy and slow at learning, the next thing I would do is to open my diary and read out to myself what I want to become and achieve before I breathe my last breath. In addition, I discovered that each time I did that my strength gets renewed. You may have to work on a strategy that helps you to re-energize yourself at some point.

It is true that some events in life are unpalatable and difficult to absorb. They have their meanings. Some of the reasons we may never know, but the bottom line is that let the gods know that there is a Supreme God behind all the gods.

Gone are the days when man used to meet with God on mountains face-to-face, with physical signs. The generation we are now requires a great deal of the work of the mind, of faith to have access to anything, be it wealth, happiness, and other desires in life. You must see it first with the "eye" of your mind before you can work your way to get at it. The mind is the most essential, most susceptible, and prevailing *tool* any man can possess, because it propagates his faith, fear, failures, ambition, vision, industriousness, and other endeavours.

Besides that, man is a complicated being with body. This body is the dwelling place of the mind, which we interpret as the spirit or soul. It is called the Soul when man is still alive, but it is called the Spirit when man is already dead. As the body of man transforms, the name transforms as well but it is still the same mind. The sharp distinction between the body and the mind is that while the body of man grows old with time, the mind grows more active, more effective, and even "younger" at the same time!

This school of thought accounts for the reason why older people are more knowledgeable as their body grows old. The increase in knowledge is like the strength of a man when he is still young. When a man is still young, he does many things with his body (which is physically strong) but when a man becomes older, he can predict the end of a matter with ease and better than the younger ones. Thanks to an African proverb, that says, *"What an elderly man lies down to see, a young man may climb the tallest tree on the tallest mountain, yet he will not see it."*

Every action or inaction of every person is an offspring of his or her thought. Your choice in every of your desires or your view in any of your situations is determined by your thoughts. Before any reasonable leap, there must be a thought to warrant the leap.

You have in you the principles of secret spiritual knowledge that can redefine your reality and teach you the art of creating miracles in your everyday life.

CHAPTER RECAPS

The mind is the real person that is living in the body. Every man is two in one - body and mind. It is only the body of man that is known by another man, for example, you know me by my name, by the sound of my voice, the shape of my head or face and so on, but the real me is only known by me, and that real me is my mind. That is why whatever anyone has to say about someone else's state of mind at any point in time is nothing but guesswork. The sixth sense (that is, the mind) is the real man, and a man's success begins there.

Chapter Ten
GIVING

Have you ever stopped to think about the origin of gift giving rituals? While you may think that gift giving isn't really that big of a deal, there is a great deal of history behind this that most people don't even really think about. The term refers to an object given by one person to another person, with regards to increasing the amount of happiness in their life, or just decreasing the amount of sadness. This can take place on special days, special occasions, and at times when a person might need a lift.

In ancient China, there was what they called *"giving before you take"* – with the impression that the giving makes it hard for the other person to notice the taking. According to Robert Green, *"giving before taking softens the ground, takes the bite out of a future request, or simply creates a distraction"*. Giving can take many forms: an actual gift, a generous act, a kind favour among others.

The fact of human nature is that every man loves gifts. A fancy gift from an enemy's camp can be enticing to a certain level. A gift is one of the perfect ways to disarm people, weaken them, cheat them, blindfold your intentions, and take over their territory. Everyone just loves gifts; that is why most deceivers and frauds use them as bait sometimes; in the form of good and mouth-watering returns. They just have one intention: to weaken you and get at you easily.

Since the dawn of time people have been giving presents. People in early civilizations gave to their tribal leaders and each other to show loyalty and love. They used bark and wood from the trees, and reeds to fashion unique objects. The Romans called it *good luck tokens.* They received presents to procure favour and to demonstrate allegiance, a practice still in place today. In Egypt, idols and pyramids were built to honour the pharaohs. In the medieval age, gifts were given to kings to gain personal favour or allegiance in a war. Most were silver and gold and jewels, which were molded into chalices, medallions, statues, and other articles. They were also given to beloved ones or used as dowries for betrothals, which could include animals, precious metals, or jewellery.

Today we give for a myriad of reasons. Presents are given at cultural/ religious occasions, for birthdays, holidays, farewells, good luck, to show love, to say thank you, to welcome. We give presents to family members, friends, co-workers, and neighbours and the selection may include jewelry, baskets, toys, clothes, certificates, flowers, and plants.

Sometimes gift giving could be in the form of rendering services. For example, children give their parents coupons for yard cleanup, help with dish washing, cleaning the house and other chores they might not ordinarily perform at some point in their lives. Some other times the gifts may be intangible but valuable); like giving time to our family, friends, and neighbours when they need help. People volunteer their time to various charitable organizations too.

Receiving is part of this process. Giving makes the giver feel good. Making someone else's life richer rewards the giver with a feeling of achievement and caring, especially if the recipient shows gratitude and appreciation. Receiving is as important in this reciprocal practice as giving.

It has symbolic meaning in nearly every culture from all corners of the globe for as long as mankind has existed. From the first time a father gave his child a carved toy to the gold ring given to a bride, gift receiving symbolizes many things: acceptance of love, respect, sympathy, flattery, and appreciation. This has become a time-honoured tradition that has become deeply rooted with time. Over time, this wonderful tradition has grown more complicated and more stressful. Sometimes, the original purpose behind the tradition gets clouded, and it takes on a life of its own.

The Holy Scriptures says that it is more blessed to give than to receive. The reason is that it is not easy to give. Whenever anyone develops the ability to give, that person has been able to demonstrate the greatest of all the basic laws that can keep the world in peace and unity and that is the law of love. Every atom of giving has an element of love attached to it, consciously or unconsciously.

In fact, anytime you give, you are sowing a seed as well. Seed must germinate, grow, and begin to produce seeds. In most cases, just as in the law of reproduction, seeds guarantee that a particular species of plant or animal continues to exist. Without the seeds growing to produce other seeds, all lives would have gone into extinction. This is the same manner the law of giving operates. The moment you stop giving, you start going into extinction. Yes. It is that serious. Some people are so good at only receiving. They love to receive but never want to reciprocate giving. The implication of it is so gravy that you can lose all respect from loved ones if you are always caught in this net. You can lose opportunities too.

There is another dimension to giving. For example, when a distant uncle of mine gave me a computer system, it was the best thing he had ever done for me since I knew him. As of then, I had no knowledge of computers. I admire people who sit in front of a computer and work with it. I desired it the same way, so I pressurized the man to please buy me a used computer. After a while, he bought it. Years later, I became so good at using the computer. He fulfilled my dream. So, a time came when he needed someone to handle some typing and graphics work, and I was the one available to do the job for him, free of charge.

The other dimension is that what you gave in the time past can as well return to begin to serve you. No wonder Late Lucky Dube says, *"be good to people on your way up the ladder because you may meet them on your way down when they will be going up."*

If you can do this always, you will never lack. A giver never lacks – because he will reap what he sowed in the lives of others.

Give and it shall be given unto you.

CHAPTER RECAP

Reciprocate giving.

We are in a world where some people will ask you "how are you" but they do not really care much about your response or responses. Some of the people may hear you talk, but they do not really listen to you; while some see you, but they never really observe you. The irony about this set of people is that they do not care much for anyone, but they want to be cared for. That is selfishness in pure form. Selfishness has ruined a lot of homes, relationships, friendship and so on. No wonder Jesus Christ admonishes his followers *to do to others what they want others to do to them.*

The law of reciprocation states that you do to others what you would them do to you. It is a basic and simple rule but when you meet its conditions, it blesses you in return or it humiliates you on the other hand. If someone does something nice to you once, say twice, do not ever wait for the third time uninterrupted by you. Begin to reciprocate, no matter how little, make sure you interrupt the chain. If possible, outdo what he/she has done for you. This way, the relationship can never end.

If you come across someone who is always taking but never giving always, get off as fast as you can. This is because such a relationship will never last! Do not always take without giving back always. The equation must be balanced for you to earn your respect and improve your impression or reputation. It is a law that must never be broken; even if it must break, let it not break in your hands.

If you want to succeed, that is one secret to imbibe.

Chapter Eleven
WILLS

Oh! Light is good. Light is life, just as truth and salt are. Everyone needs light. Everyone needs nothing but the truth. Everyone needs salt to live. At any point in your life, you need a glimpse of light, the truth, and a little salt to make your life meaningful.

It is not surprising therefore, that Christ likened his followers to light and salt and himself the truth. In all life's pursuit, we all need these facts for personal development and interactions with one another.

Similarly, many people desire money, a loving home, academic qualifications, peace of mind, wealth, forgiveness, power; love etc. if not all of these, then most of them. However, these things are not available to anyone in full. For those that seek for money or wealth for instance, God does not rain down manna from heaven anymore, rather he said; *"the work of your hands I shall bless"*. However, there is more to working and getting blessed. To work means to bridge your ideas to your realities. But you must first see the realities of tomorrow from today. These are the first requirements - dreams and visions- the products of the mind.

Now, our Creator respects, marvels and appreciates our imaginations and wills. For example, before now, the entire world was of one language. When the people as that time made up their minds to build a tower to reach unto heavens, God himself confessed to the power of their imaginations, wills, and unity. I wonder how they did it because the distance between the earth and the sun where I may ignorantly call the heavens, is over 93 million miles but they did it!

"And the whole earth was of one language, and of one speech. And it happened, as they journeyed from the east, that they found a plain in the land of Shinar; and they dwelt there. And they said one to another, go to, let us make brick, and burn them thoroughly. And they had brick for stone, and slime for mortar. And they said, go to, let us build us a city and a tower, whose top may reach unto heaven; and

let us make us a name, lest we be scattered abroad upon the face of the whole earth. And the LORD came down to see the city and the tower, which the children of men built.

And the LORD said, Behold, the people is one, and they have all one language; and this they begin to do: and now nothing will be restrained from them, which they have imagined doing. (Genesis 11)"

It is very consoling to know that our Creator respects our wills. Nothing will he withhold from anyone who has a will. It does not really matter who the person is. It does not matter where you come from. When you have wills to get up to achieve or to get something done, then God is close by you. Where there is a will, there is a way. And where there is a way, there is God because, God is the way.

Now, it is one thing to have dreams and visions, but it is entirely another thing for people to accept you and your visions. If you want to win, after every mental plan, the next thing you need is the will to rise and start. Starting is always the most difficult of every meaningful project because many things will still be in their raw state, void and meaningless. This is the point many dreams and glorious world-changing visions are buried. Yes! At this stage, people will no longer regard you as a normal person for daring big projects. And even if they do, they will give your vision reasons why it is 'impossible' for it to become a reality. At this stage, they will list imperceptible people who have attempted such vision and how they all failed. And at this stage they will tell you how the economy will not favour your visions just because you may ask them for financial assistance.

I believe even if others have attempted it before and they all failed, it does not mean it cannot be done by another person. It is possible that the people who did it and failed never gave their best or they never saw light in their failures that could lead them through their dream(s) from another point. It could be some other factors beyond their immediate control and so on. But do those factors signify impossibility? There are no impossibilities anywhere.

When Marconi Guglielmo, an Italian Physicist dreamt of a system that could harness the intangible forces of the ether for the invention of a wireless telegraphy, experts condemned him saying, it would not work! In fact, he was repeating Hertz's experiment (Hertz is another scientist of the same kind as Marconi), but in another way. Experts condemned him and even his friends took him to a psychiatrist hospital to ascertain the status of his mental fitness when he formerly announced his proposed project. Upon all this, Marconi was seeing something that his friends could not see. That thing was light at the end of the tunnel fueled by the will to either attempt it or die instead. His wireless telegraphy has now made people of all nations become back-door neighbours. Today, radios and similar facilities of Marconi have transformed the world into a global village.

The good thing is that when you eventually breakthrough, the people who condemned your ideas, will come up to make use of the same idea saying, "we thought it was impossible." Shame on all dream killers! Dreamers and visionaries must understand at this point that one of the signs that could point to the usefulness of any idea is chronic oppositions- by those who do not have the will, the ability and faith to see and believe your ideas. In all, never give up your dreams. Do something about it whether it worked or not. The generations to come may pick it up someday to achieve it for you. If what you wish to do is right, you never give it up.

According to the Late Chief Gani Fawehinmi, the founder and presidential candidates of National Conscience Party, a Senior Advocate of Nigeria and a Human Rights Activist, every right-thinking person must *"stand up for what is right, even if you are standing alone"*. The only friend, strength and hope you need to stand for what you believe in, is your will!

The Wright Brothers (Wilbur and Orville Wrights, Americans) faced the same problem when they came up with the idea of a machine that can fly.

When a Doctor Falls Ill

Today the airplane is one of the prides of modern civilizations. Many people came up to advocate and broaden theories that what is heavier than air cannot stay in the air, it must fall because they threw a stone into the air, and it fell. Today, not only does that *bird machine* which is far heavier than air flies in the air, it carries many people and luggage in its flight. Surprisingly, those who faulted the idea will come into the plane and say, 'we thought it would not work.'

The same way, Thomas Edison dreamt of a lamp that can be operated by electricity. After several failures and oppositions, today we now have fluorescent tubes in banks, homes, airports, on the streets, schools and anywhere human beings can be found – being powered by electricity comfortably.

Finally, Martin Luther King Jr. had a dream that someday a black America will become president of American and that dream came true when president, Barrack Obama was sworn in as American's first ever black president.

Your dreams and visions may not serve the people of your generation, still don't give it up. It is a legacy you must leave behind.

All the people described above had the choice to forget about their dreams because of the oppositions but they never did. That brings us to the fact that life is what you make of it. You have the willpower to choose and not to. You have the choice to agree with opposition and move on as a person who takes 'wise' counsels. But when you become poor without anything to your name, the same people who condemned your dreams and vision and made them appear impossible, will mock you saying, 'you are a failure, where were you when your folks made it'?

CHAPTER RECAP

Everyone thinks he or she has the will to do anything all the time but behold only a few and the great ones among them think and do! The law of wills states that until you rise to your challenges, until you rise to the task, until you attempt to move something, nothing will move! Every object on all the planets wants stability. Only you know the stable point. Never give up your dreams! Why, because your dreams and visions are your life – minus them, you are dead, technically.

Chapter Twelve
SUCCESS

"Success has many friends", is a popular phrase.

In Nigeria and other countries around the world, every month and year, churches dish out prophetic tags for their members for the month or year. Tags like "My year of abundance," "Year of fruitfulness," "From glory to glory," "My case is different" etc. are common.

There are possibilities that most members will remain the same.

Though there are no specific evaluation mechanisms that can measure the outcome of these prophetic tags, it is obvious in some cases, that such tags do not produce the effect as much as they sound to the ears.

This is because what is required for effective and positive impacts are not the tags but what the people do with the contents of the tags. This is where the battle line is often drawn.

When a Doctor Falls Ill

The reason many of us have not achieved much in life is that we are comfortable with what we already have. We all know that it is a good moral characteristic for one to be contented. However, in a situation where one is living in lack, poverty, bondage and stagnation, no man should be contented with that. Throw away this moral value, at least, at this point, because it is not God's will for anyone to boast in poverty and lack. That is to say that it is only when you have become fed up with where you are that you are likely to take the step required to move to the next level. Something new would happen when you make such a move.

For example, imagine that the wife of a chain cigarette smoker hides all materials that can light up a stick of cigarette in the house.

"Just to stop him from smoking; smoking is dangerous to health" she reasoned.

Imagine also that the man is now ready to have a stick and he finds nothing to light it up. But he is determined to take a stick. Remember, he is a chain smoker. Believe me, a new method of lighting a stick of cigarette will be discovered. Do you know why? *Necessity is the mother of invention!* When you earnestly need a thing, I mean earnestly, that is when your change will come. It is not greed; it is about desire for a necessity.

Your success does not start when you begin to see the manifestations of your thought, it starts the moment you can conceive a profitable idea. That point is the moment you become earnestly determined to become the success you dreamt of. That is when your success begins.

Success has two ends: One is your preparation after the initial conception, the other is the recognition of an opportunity. The art is to ensure that preparation and the opportunity can meets.

In the words of Pastor Ayo Orisejafor, *divine blessing is when opportunity meets preparation.*

Napoleon Hill, the author of a widely read book titled *'Think and Grow Rich'* pointed out that every human being who reaches the age of understanding the purpose of money wishes for it. Unfortunately, wishes alone aren't enough. We know that getting the money in the real bank requires action or series of actions called work.

Those who have succeeded in life are those who have first succeeded in their minds.

Somebody may be asking, why is it that some people do think of good things about themselves and yet such things do not come their way? Well, the answer is here. It is important to mention that there is nothing a man can think of that he cannot do or achieve in this life. It all depends on you, to decide whether you want it exactly the way you thought of it, you want it close, or you do not want it at all but just like thinking of it.

It is believed that genius experiments every of their thoughts to find out why such thoughts came to their minds in the first place. No wonder they are geniuses! When you think, you must do something to get a result out of it. Thinking alone is not enough! Everyone is thinking. It is a general thing. It is only those that "do" after the general thinking that can attain greatness. This is like faith and work. Faith is only effective when you work; hence, faith without work is dead.

Everything you have in your life is a direct result of your thoughts, both conscious and subconscious (visions and dreams respectively). If you do not have everything you want in your life, then it may be time to get out of the "usual" process you are already used to, so that you can focus that power on getting exactly what you want.

To make this important change, you may have to change your environment, your decision, or ensure you meet the conditions of natural or universal laws (terms and conditions).

When a Doctor Falls Ill

There exists a thin line with short or long processes between what you think in your mind and the possibility of those things happening to you. That thin line is called ACTION. Action is the secret behind what many people call luck. Action if rightly taken creates room for luck and success. An action they say speaks louder than words upon words. For example, you are imagining that a piece of item at a distance from you, should be in your hand. Imagine the item to be a treasure. After imagining it lifting itself, moving towards you and then dropping in your hands, you will discover that it is still where it was. You will not be holding it, even though you have thought of it moving towards you bit by bit like someone taking steps and then finally into your hands.

All that notwithstanding, it will not be in your hands. Why? Why was your thought not able to move it? It is because thinking alone is not enough!

Action is required!

Yes! The treasure, or whatever it is you are looking for, will not come unless you, or someone or something, moves it. Precisely, you that needed it have not moved it so it will not move into your hand as you have imagined it.

For the target to get to you, action is required, or series of actions are required. One of which may be that you take physical steps towards it. You may need to build new relationships, offer to help someone that matters within the domain of your target, seek professional training, step up your game or packaging to attract the target, take an examination, partner with someone, and so on.

If you have some supernatural means, you could remain where you are, call on someone to go to do all those actions for you.

Whichever way you choose, action or actions are required by you to get the work done. It is that "will" to act, that differentiates one person from another. Some will want to wait for "others" to open the way, then they can follow, but how many followers have you heard their names in the books of records? You can be the pacesetter!

Waiting for others to "open the gates", is one of the silent ways in which nothing gets done quickly or timely. This is because calling on someone to do the action for you, especially if the idea is a fresh one, requires you to first convey your thoughts to the person, ensuring that he or she has the same picture of what you want to do. This later action can delay the actualization of your idea because everyone is loaded with one problem or the other bothering them. They may not "catch" your vision clearly. And that is a huge problem.

Some years ago, I brought some goods to sell to my fellow students in school. Because I was living off campus, some students I spoke to agreed to help me sell some of the items in the hostels at a commission. To one, I gave 22 pieces, to another I gave 30 while I kept 50 for myself. Two weeks later, I exhausted the 50 with me but to my greatest surprise and disappointment, the one I gave 22 had only sold one. The person with 30, what did he do? He first complained that the 30 was 29 and he too had sold only one! Do the action yourself my friend if you want the best out of your fresh ideas. The initial start-up requires that you be fully involved. That will be a reasonable thing to do. Later, you could use technology to engage people and still be in control.

For you to get what you want out of life, you must do something. To come out with this book, I must sit and write! That you want to be a professor requires that you go to school, pass all your courses, and do all that is required of you before you can profess. If you want to climb higher on the ladder of your chosen profession, you must contribute to it with new and functional ideas. Note that it is ideas that are backed-up with actions that are ruling the world.

Some people are only imagining their own contribution to the growth of the company where they work. If you are in that category, please go voice out your ideas in writing. Writing will make it very formal.

If you do not say it out, nobody knows that you've any contribution to make.

Similarly, if you want to work and get paid by someone, you must go out there and search for it. You must send out as many applications as possible, and don't get put off by disappointing outcomes.

If the job is not available and you really need a job to do, then you've got to create one.

"The work of your hand I shall bless", says the Holy Scripture.

You must do something to bring the picture in you to reality. If yours is such that you want to belong to the set of gods that go to the office when they like, then you've to work hard to own the office. To be called a leader, you must lead properly. To own an office, you must work hard and smart for it.

Often, you hear people say, 'I thought I told you about it.' 'Didn't I tell you I was traveling'? 'I had in mind to inform you and I thought I did.' Such comments come up when someone fails to perform certain actions, he/she had imagined, hence no realities. This is because you never opened your mouth to voice out your thoughts and as a result, the person never got the picture in your mind. That is, he or she was not told!

Something always goes wrong when you fail to take an action where an action is required. One of which is that your dream company may never be known by anyone except you!

Many people have lost many things in life for not acting when an action is required. For example, you do not go praying in church when you are supposed to be at work or be preparing for an exam. You must have to work on things to work out for you.

Examining a king called King David in the Bible, it was recorded that *when kings were supposed to be at the war front* (ACTION), he was at home.

What happened? He saw a woman, the wife of one of his soldiers taking her bath. He sent for her and

When a Doctor Falls Ill

went into her. What were the results? Atrocities, murder, and punishments! The result of such inaction is that there can never be a positive reality.

In life, nothing moves unless someone or something moves it. When you back your thoughts with wheels of actions, you are bound to see something happen.

The amazing thing about Universal Laws is that even if a criminal applies its principles, it will still work out something for him or her! Every idea backed up with action is equal to result – either good or bad.

If there is anything on earth called good luck, then it awaits those who are ready to accept responsibility and opportunity. To have a successful home, a successful business, you must act now. If you don't, nothing will happen, luck may come and opportunity may come but because you are not ready to act, when they come, you wouldn't even know.

You are the master of your dreams, so go do something yourself to bring your dreams to reality. Real testimonies come to those who back their thoughts with actions. The reason is that for you to get to the other side of the river, you must cross the bridge. Those who wish to be on the other side of the bridge without them taking the action of crossing the bridge can only live on fantasies.

Crossing over to the other side is only for those who have ideas and are determined to bring them to reality. It is for those who see their present low condition in life as not matching their godly status. Crossing over is for those who have realized and are fed up with their condition and desires a change!

Yes! You'll dwell on fantasies if you are not ready to act by doing something to invoke positive changes in your finances, marriage and even academic or work performances. You can only continue to dream but no achievements unless you hook up with the centre - ACTION!

Even biblically, Christ is the medium through which Christians can reach God. He is the mediator between God and man. To get to the Creator requires only one way. For Christians, Christ is that bridge they must cross, the saviour they must trust and accept before they can reach God.

The same way, actions connect us with our realities. The fact that you could think of a particular idea could mean or signify that you can make it real.

A popular commercial bank once put up an advert that reads:

'People think. Great people think and do it.'

That is thoughtful and very correct, because everyone is thinking it, but not everyone is doing it. That alone accounts for differences in social status among people of all races and colours. Anything that does not require action takes you nowhere. Action means doing something to an existing thing to get a better or an improved result or doing something entirely new.

Action is a deliberate effort, and the secret tool that great often used. I may say that lack of knowledge of this secret is the foundation of poverty. Some poor people may even know this secret, but they do not have the guts to make the needed moves. "What if I lose my money or my life", they may reason.

Ordinary people only think. But Great people think it and do it.

Do you know that the great people that you see around don't lie about at home and enjoy food and drinks as we presume them to be doing? In fact, before you get prepared in the morning to go find your daily bread, they have gone far into the day. And even when you think it is time to get home and rest, they could be somewhere making moves for tomorrow's gains.

Now, weigh yourself! Have you ever actualized a thought? Then, greatness is in you. The more you actualize your thoughts, the more your greatness becomes noticed and pronounced. A drop of water can make a sea when we have several drops; the same way, bits of greatness or achieved dreams or thoughts, can make your greatness pronounce.

Every man is born great.

The potential, the energy, the zeal, the desire, and all that you need to make things happen are inside of you. They are in that breath that made a man a living soul. Study yourself closely and you'll find out that you are one of the gods' that God uses to make the world a better place.

There is something you can do with ease that others cannot. That is one of the sources of your greatness and wealth. Search yourself repeatedly.

This zeal is in-born but you've got to do something, something called Action.

I know I have said enough on this, but there is no better way to drum up this secret than to exemplify it as much as possible.

The sketch below can further explain the Idea-Action-Reality of the law of success.

```
┌─────────┐        ┌─────────┐
│  IDEAS  │──▶ ACTION(s) ──▶│REALITIES│
└─────────┘        └─────────┘
```

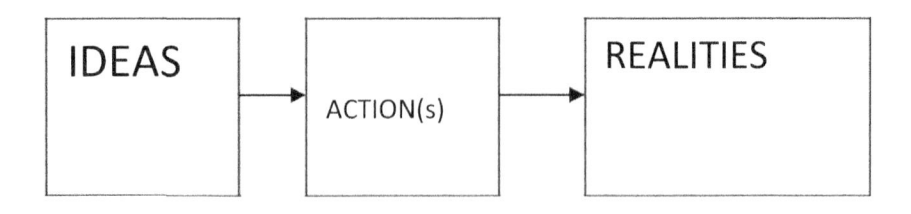

You cannot get to reality from ideas unless you pass through action or actions. No flying over in this game of life. No other way, no shortcut, because something must be done for a new thing to come to life. Many people want to jump over action into reality, where they can begin to enjoy life, but it can never be so unless you want blood on your hands!

Taking a planned action is hard, and the hard way is always the often way.

Great people dare almost all their ideas. It may be checked by some failures or disappointments here and there, but lessons are learnt in each case. Remember that obstacles and failures are meant to make us better and move forward.

Now consider the floating sketch another way as below:

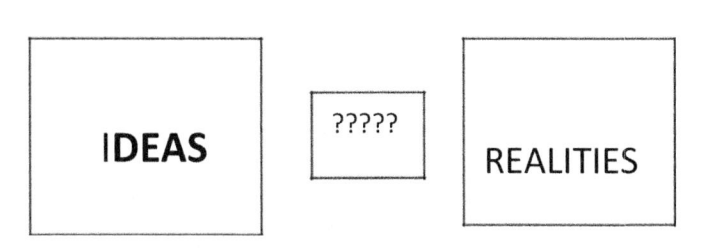

| IDEAS | ????? | REALITIES |

Ideas and realities have no links without a mediator but unfortunately, this is where many people are found. We have ideas, loads of ideas, great ideas indeed but no action to join you in your realities. In fact, you see the ideas as if they are already real, only for you to come back to yourself after a deep thought that you are still where you were - possibly in your bed. Get up my dear and create a joint between your ideas and your world. Nothing happens unless you make it happen! Even a prayer does not have potency without action.

Ideas that are backed up with actions are the ingredients that are ruling the world today. So, you must open a way for others to follow. Yes. You can open the way for others to follow. Those who dare to open a way are usually the celebrated few of society.

I was listening to an advert on the radio one day that talked about a scratch card that one can buy and search for jobs from the notable companies around. I heard one voice that struck my mind, and it says: 'you can have all the information about the companies of your choice in Nigeria, so get the card at ABC bank…. And begin to apply today.'

Suddenly, an unseen force lifted me up from my bed immediately and I asked myself 'who owns the companies?' By this time, I was already standing with my two hands holding my waist and my eyes staring at the radio set. I was expecting an answer from someone but all I could hear was silence.

After which, I heard a still small voice saying; "Men like you own the companies!" I can hear the same voice talking to you right now that "you can own the companies". Help others. Open the gates. Be a pacesetter.

Someone sat down one day, created out a company name from names and then gave it actions. That was how a place where people work and get paid was built. I cannot explain what happened to me that day, but I was very sure I visited another world.

Of course, you can also be successful as an employee. I have said enough on that already, and the summary of it is that you should be an employee with ideas. Present the ideas formally and see how your career will take off.

What is it that you desire? If it is a successful marriage for instance, what have you done about it? A wise man once said that love between married couples is like a burning wood. It usually burns high in flames initially when the wood is still much; but the moment the wood gets burnt off the fire begins to go down.

So, what do you do then? The wise man is still saying you should add more woods. Are you adding more woods? Always think of the thing that made you marry your spouse in the first place.

Reignite the passion as often as you can because the truth is that, even if you move in with another spouse, there is the same probability that you would get fed up repeatedly unless you keep adding more wood to your initial setup.

Perhaps yours is not marriage but business, what are you doing about it? Will you continue to sit and imagine for years without action? Yes, it's hard these days getting financial support for either business or research; but then, even if it means contacting every person on earth before your desire can be achieved, please do it.

It is better to try and fail and try again than not to even try at all.

The fact that somebody says he cannot support you today does not mean he will not support you another day. In most cases, they want to know how serious, realistic, and desirous you are about your idea. They have the cash for genuine business, but they can only offer the cash to a genuine idea that can make them increase their cash. That one is sure for all money owners. It's now left for you to prove your understanding of what you want to do in proposals and practical projections. Imagine someone asking for a million naira from you for a particular business you've no idea of. Will you give me the money?

The reality is that it is not easy to give out money because it is hard to make it. In a recent interview with CNN in Washington, Jeff Bezos said this about charity and philanthropy.

"It's not easy. Building Amazon was not easy. It took a lot of hard work, a bunch of very smart teammates, hard-working teammates, and I'm finding… that charity, philanthropy, is very similar."

If you want money for your ideas, present valid arguments, and projections.

What are you still doing down there? You are down there complaining that something is not done right and perhaps you are even asking if there is nobody who can do anything about it. If nobody is doing something about a thing and you are somebody, why are you still down there? You can think or imagine the solution but if you do nothing about it, it will remain unsolved.

You want a good life, then get up and cross the bridge. Get up to the other side. The other side is where those who had guts lived after they were able to cross over the bridge. The name of the bridge remains ACTION.

Action speaks louder than words they say, and no law can stand against that.

I was traveling some time ago and there was an accident along my route, the two vehicles involved in the accident totally blocked the entire highway. As busy as the highway was, all the vehicles from both sides only came to that point to join the long queue.

When the bus I was in came, we joined the waiting people and vehicles as well. I said to myself, unless we do something, we will remain like this till night falls, and that could be dangerous for all of us, considering the remoteness of the scene of accident. My fellow travelers were asking me if I could push the trailers off the road, mockingly. Some were suggesting we wait for Road Safety Personnel to come first and clear the way.

Of course, I could not push trailers off the highway (no one can), but I could do something else.

"Rocks are broken with skills not with strength." Plus, I strongly believe that when one road closes in life, another must have opened somewhere. God cannot, at any point in time leave us without alternatives.

Like a joke, those who believed my words joined me in the adventure and before the rest knew what was happening, we formed a new 'highway' through the bush path! All I was hearing was, "he did it"!

I became a hero on the spot after some people who had waited for over four hours, now had access to move. If I had wanted, every vehicle that wanted to take "my highway" to pay a fine, many, if not all, would have gladly paid. My friend, go start something.

Finally, in the words of John Crowe, *it takes a strong fish to swim against the current. Even a dead one can float with it.*

Get up and get it done. In the world of today, if you don't look out for a problem in one area to solve, don't expect your daily bread. Do not be afraid of failure, because it is a step forward to the next level. Failure is like discovering a new way that something cannot be done. Act. Now!

CHAPTER RECAP

People think all the time, but only great people think and do. We have had a lot of political, social, and even religious reform programmes over the years, but because there are no implementations of the programs (which is equivalent to taking actions on ideas), you discover that the governments are doing the same thing repeatedly over the years – alas, on paper! They make laws but never implemented them; and even if they implement, they do it partially for a while and forget about it when they return to break the laws to their own selfish advantage.

Many of the people you come across on the streets are thinking of one thing or the other to do to make their lives better, but only a few "do" what it takes to make their thoughts a reality. The majority gives up to challenges, setbacks, discouragement, failure, difficulty, blurred vision and so on. But the little few, who also experience all the difficulties mentioned above see beyond the challenges and the difficulties. They see light at the end of the tunnel; and they are the gods. They are the gods of our time because they are not driven by their difficulties, but they are driven by their dreams and visions.

They are not driven by the losses they encounter during their "doing or actioning" an idea, they are driven by the ideas that make them start the entire process. They are aware that nothing works unless someone makes it work. It is a devilish lie that God blesses someone who do not carry out his assignment or work well. He said that the work of your hands I shall bless, therefore whoever does not work (action), may never be blessed. In fact, at some point, it is said that whoever does not work, should not eat!

Imagine someone working in a company where he sleeps all day in the office when they are files he ought to attend to. He can't be blessed; he will have trouble instead of promotion and pay rise. Praying cannot solve the problems unless you back it up with work.

While preparing for my Senior School Certificate Examinations (SSCE), my father once told me that after the exams, he will be sending me to a College of Education. According to him, University was not for someone like me. The fact that he belittled "College of Education" worried me then and even now. Inside of me, I knew he did not know my strengths.

I had brought my termly results (report card) to him many times, he refused to look at them. He did not even collect the report card from my hand. He then said to me, "if you are doing great in your school, then your school is really a backward school". I stopped attempting to have him look at my report card from that moment onward.

Before the SSCE results came out in 2001, he had sent me packing to the village. My offence was that I started a "Home to Home" car wash business. I was washing cars for people around my neighbourhood for cash. He said I dishonoured him with that move. One morning, he pounced on me, dragging me into his car and straight to the motor park. I travelled a whole day, covering over 400KM back to my village. The nicker I went to bed with the previous night, and a bathroom slipper, along with some of my belongings in carrier bags, were all I had.

And when the results came out, I was among the top students in the school, according to the West African Examination Council that authenticated the SSCE.

Do I care what his thoughts about me now? Nope. I have created my own path and moved on.

What happens if things don't work out as planned? Read on.

Chapter Thirteen
WHEN MAN IS TO BLAME

Those who live in a glass house should not be throwing stones. The reason is that when they do, they will end up with broken walls (glasses), and they will become vulnerable to the elements outside.

"All organisms, [including humans], are greatly influenced by the consequences produced by their own behaviour (B.F. Skinner, 1938 in *The Behaviour of Organisms*).

Man has always been a faultfinder from his very first home, the Garden of Eden. He does this by shifting responsibility to someone else or by exercising his mind to see whom he could nail his problems on.

It is natural that when a man sense something in his mind, he tends to link what he has sensed with other possibilities, to arrive at a concrete conclusion. In such a case, the mindset of the individual before the event determines which direction, he would channel his or her thoughts.

In other words, I am what you envisage me to be.

If you do not envisage me to be a right-thinking personality, no matter what I do, plausible or not, you would still see me as you usually do. It takes courage to accept defeat. It will take courage to re-organize our long-held opinions or traditions. Peradventure I am good and yet you still see me as bad, it means that we are just *natural enemies*, of which one or all the people involved are responsible.

There is only one consciousness in the world, and that is at every individual's level. That consciousness is your own. You treat others as your consciousness tells you; and others treat you as their consciousness tells them. This can result in natural conflict and the only solution is for the people concerned to clean up their consciousness.

The environment influences every individual differently; the influence can be positive or negative or both. However, the worrisome effects are that it could make innocent people suffer along with the guilty (and sometimes without the guilty) over sins or errors committed by the guilty.

During a youth gathering in a local church some years back, we were having an open discussion tagged, "Say Your Mind". Everyone presents had an opportunity to say their minds on any issue. The topic of discussion that day was *fairness.*

Some of us wanted to know why life seems fair to some and unfair to others. Different people were in the hall that day, young doctors, lawyers, engineers, bricklayers, farmers, teachers, and other fields of endeavours. An exclusive banter of the mind was going on as some persons reasoned that God or Nature is a bit partial with its activities on earth while others reasoned otherwise. Some asked where God was when innocent people get punished.

This was going on when suddenly a child that followed one of the participants to the meeting defecated. Everyone in the hall became uncomfortable, not even the doctors could help, nor the pastors.

No one could stand the smell, and some developed serious stomach aches from the smell while others managed to throw away saliva that had naturally gathered in their mouths.

The discussion then took a sharp turn when someone asked the gathering to know what every one of us in the hall had done wrong to deserve the smell that was not caused by any of us. Why is it that the smell does not channel its flow to the one who defecated but instead distributed itself to everyone in the room?

The present Egyptians should also be asking similar questions on why God chose to use them as scapegoats for the Israelites.

There is just one reason for this. Every one of us is vulnerable to challenges or problems facing other people around us. Troubles await anyone who finds himself on the surface of the earth. You may and may not be the cause of the problem, yet you will be part of the consequences if, for any reason, you find yourself within the receiving environment.

No wonder a writer once pointed out that at any point in time, you are either coming out of one trouble, or you are about entering one or you are right in one and making efforts to find your way out-to get into another again. The same reasoning goes, when you've a tyre failure on a highway, or when your car breaks down. It could have been the error of the mechanic, or the manufacturer of the tyre or even the car itself, but you are the one suffering the failures.

The environment we live in and the fact that we deal with other people every day leads to our own pains or gains. It can be disheartening or rewarding. There is a constant temptation to judge.

Now, are occurrences such as failures, breakdowns, and other similar unpleasant events of life because of one's sin or error?

Not always.

Even the son of God was killed unjustly. That you fail does not make you a failure or a sinner because it could have happened to anyone. It happened to you because you were in the receiving environment.

The big thing in all life('s) problems is the ability to find out why the problem came so that it does not repeat itself in later time. You would no longer be a victim anymore if you could learn a lesson from it. You can learn to stay away from the receiving environment. You can even learn to shield yourself from the receiving environment. This way, you would have fewer pains and more gains in life.

For example, I told a story before about a man who spent two years in prison awaiting trial because he went to watch football games where criminals also watch sport activities. After hearing this story, I need not an angel to appear to me before I knew that the place was a *no-go area*. I thank God I did not learn the hard way. You don't have to. If I was adamant in such a situation, I could have been a victim. No one would have been blamed but me.

When a Doctor Falls Ill

It may interest you to know that the receiving environment is the reason why a doctor can fall ill. It may also interest you to know that the problems facing humanity, is man himself. What do we expect God to do when we pick up a knife to stab ourselves or someone else? Can a man hold a burning coal in his palms and not get burnt? Can he sit on a burning coal and not get hurt? Proverbs 6 v 28.

People always have reasons to do what they do. However, the problem is how reasonable are the reasons? How reasonable are your reasons for failing? How reasonable are your reasons to beat up your wife and send her away because of another woman? How reasonable are your reasons for that singular act of yours that is impoverishing the entire nation just because of you and your family? How reasonable are they? If you've no reason to do what you are doing, then you've no *reasoning.* That is my opinion.

If at any point in time you find yourself doing certain things under the pretence that some persons are influencing you, it is because you've loved to do that thing first in your mind. The principles you live on, or the guiding force behind what you do, the judgments you give to any event in your life are a product of your thought. The view of your mind determines the solution you can offer to any situation that you find yourself.

There was a story of a man in the village I partly grew up, who went after prostitutes to satisfy his sexual desires. He had two wives and several children at home at this point. He was not of that nature until he bought a Peugeot 504. More women were trooping in to have their share of him. Of course, he was willingly giving it to them. Months after months passed, and the same prostitutes ended up killing him in a fight on who should be with the man. He did not even enjoy the car as much as he ought to. What do we expect of God in this case? In my opinion, there is nothing! The freedom that God has given us, we can use it or misuse it. Man is to blame.

He died leaving his wives and children to face so many uncertainties and hardship. Did the children do anything wrong in this case? Not at all. But they are reaping the consequences because they are at the receiving end.

The receiving environment is the reason why many things don't go as planned. You have your plans; others have their own plans that can potentially influence your plans.

The environment is the reason why a genuine pastor can still have some difficulties, pains, attacks, accidents and even death. It is the reason why some of us are still barren, even though we have put everything right with God. Man is to blame because if he chooses to behave perfectly and normally too, the environment will become conducive for him to live longer and better. Remember, that a believer or an unbeliever is not going to live better or longer because he or she is a believer or an unbeliever in God. If your behaviour is anti-life, you may not live long.

When a Doctor Falls Ill

Sometimes ago in one small village, one reckless young man was driving aimlessly as he was purposely driving to amuse his friends who were with him in the car. As he sped and stopped sporadically, they clapped and cheered him up to "ride on"! Many people were watching, and some were even "cheering" him up with handclaps.

"I wonder how these children get driving license from the government these days", an elderly man who was also watching the scene, lamented. "The young man behind that wheel has no reason whatsoever to have a driving license". But in a country where people take laws into their hands, no one could raise objections, in case the young man would come after them. He continued recklessly, going up and downtown with one of the latest jeeps at that time until he ran into a young girl, Afshatu, that was selling oranges along the road.

Now, if the recklessness had remained with him and his cycle of friends, or their own "world", no one would have bothered much. In fact, I would not have thought of penning these lines down in this book as well. However, when Afshatu's legs were later to be amputated, then, everyone became bothered.

She had her two legs amputated, thereby confining her to a wheelchair for life, because of someone else's lifestyle. The young girl was only struggling for her daily bread, since her parents and perhaps, the government had failed her at her tender age of 10 or so when she was knocked down.

The most painful aspect was that the parents of the boy swept the matter under the carpet. And that was all! Just like that, and forever she would remain lamed and caged in a wheelchair. Where was God? God is always there. He was observing everything but dominion and freedom to make choices now belongs to us (humans). That is why he (God) appear silent over some serious issues of our lives. Man is to blame.

Many of us have at one time or the other confronted some terrible challenges. Many times, we do not just know where we had gone wrong, yet some certain things just keep happening to us and keep us in a corner where the only solution left on board to consider is that of supernatural origin. Even at the supernatural end, we still have some questions. At some points, you may not even know who to blame - God or yourself or even someone else.

Now, from the Universal Laws, you can see that nothing just happened unless someone or something causes it to happen. And if something happens, it usually causes one or more things to either go right or wrong. At such points, those that are within the receiving environment (whether you are the cause or not) will reap the outcome of such events, be it good or bad. The environment therefore becomes one of the main reasons why some people suffer for sins, errors, or omissions that they are not the cause. Your environment can even kill your dream. This is an aspect of the Universal Law of cause and effect. It is a critical law.

When a Doctor Falls Ill

When a newborn baby is dumped somewhere in the toilet, gutter, roadside or even in the marketplace, you'll then ask "what had the little child done wrong to be welcomed into this world with such inhuman treatment by those who were supposed to protect it? You may as well ask God why he gave such people such children if he knows they have no capacity or love to care. That is to open your mind to the fact that since God gave man the dominion over the earth, we were placed under these laws. Whichever of the laws that you obey, you get the reward or the reproach. When you meet the conditions to reproduce, you start reproducing. It doesn't matter if you've food to feed yourself and the offspring.

In all these, however, he that is doing good, let him continue to do good, in due season, there will be some rewards. This world is not our permanent home. All the advancement in science has not been able to stop humans from dying. I believe we are still evolving. Once we were just fluids, grew within a "world" called womb, and then we found ourselves in a larger open world. It appears that death in this open world is a transformation too.

CHAPTER RECAPS

Learning from one's mistakes is one of the characters of the gods. The gods are not super humans but humans with positive attitudes and wisdom. Let life go on and keep learning from the experiences but never forget to apply wisdom that God has given you to preserve yourself from some problems that are likely to occur at every stage of your life.

Now, does the grass appear greener on the other side in your sight? If yes, look again. Your side may even be greener! The successful people you think have no single problems, sometimes confront some tougher issues than you think. But the reason why you see them as successful is because they understand their environments, face situations of life head on and ensure that they overcome any obstacle in the path.

When a Doctor Falls Ill

Truly, they feel the pains, the deaths and diseases that are ravaging the world today, but their mind is always focusing on the positive side of it all. It is true we cannot completely get rid of negative or malevolent thoughts and occurrences, but the way we respond to them often determines the outcome it will have on our physical and mental states. It is better however to avoid negative thoughts as much as possible.

'I like thinking big. I always have. To me it's very simple: If you're going to be thinking anyway,
you might as well think big.' – Donald J. Trump.

Chapter Fourteen
WHEN GOD IS TO BLAME

Seriously, you have done all you can possibly do; you had even prayed, fasted, worked, gave generously to man and to God. In fact, you have worked on yourself so much that you have killed *the old man* in you. You did all this genuinely without pretence and yet no solution to your problems. Then, many things begin to manifest in your mind; the centre of your being as regards to how God demonstrates his own kind of love.

At a certain point, your mind begins to suggest a whole lot to you. This is normal but before it suggests for you to give it up, think about this possibility: God may be the one to blame and not you!

Joseph, a promising child of his parents, the last of the twelve children that Jacob had, with his beautiful dreams, his own brothers became his "enemies". The enemies are in quote because God had made it so to affect their own lives many years later. I know, and I am very sure that ordinarily, the brothers will not have attempted such a thing just because of a dream that they do not know when and how it would manifest. However, from the reactions of the parents and even the brothers, you could see them displaying the number one problem that is tearing the whole world and causing problems for mankind:

Selfishness.

All of them were wishing they could be the one dreaming such dreams, or at least, it should be Ruben, the eldest one or better still, their father and not Joseph the beloved son of their father.

How can this small boy be the most loved and yet dreaming this kind of big dream?

"Here comes the dreamer", they said to one another, "let us kill him and see what will become of his dreams". He will not rule over us, never! They conspired but what they did not know was that they were about to push Joseph to his very place.

God has plan for Joseph in the future.

They envied him more and more as his dreams kept proving that he was indeed on a mission. At a point, in genesis 37:11, the father had to rebuke him, but he knew that God was about to do something, so he kept the matter in his mind.

Because they (the brothers) were *divinely* selfish, they chose to enrich themselves by selling off Joseph (and his dreams), but God has his own plans from the beginning of time. He knew that famine and hunger will come upon the land of Israel and there will be plenty in Egypt at the same time, so someone must go in time to prepare a place for the members of the family.

Ordinarily, as at then, the land of Israel and that of Egypt were not best of friends; so, Joseph could not have left his father's house to Egypt just because he had a dream. He did not know clearly what the dream was about. Therefore, God had to make a way for himself.

That could have been the reason Joseph was created in the first place. Even the parents were not aware of this plan; his brothers were not aware either. Even Joseph himself was not aware of where the dream will manifest. He was only dreaming. The brothers never considered how beautiful it could be to see their brother as the king or whatever God had in mind. Instead, they were concentrating on the fact that he might one day rule over them or be ahead of them.

To tell you that God's hand was working it out, when they dropped him in the pit, God was saying no, he needs to get to Egypt quickly, learn the way of Egypt from the very bottom, and later fulfill his obligations at the very top.

Therefore, Ruben became a deliverer, having a different thought and said no; "shed no blood", he said.

Being the eldest of all, they obeyed and miraculously, the Ishmaelite was passing by. In the realm of the spirit, Joseph's *train or flight* to Egypt had come.

God is to blame.

Joseph committed no sin by dreaming his *God-given* dreams, but he was on his throne watching when Joseph was maltreated and then sold. It was His plan.

The woman, Hannah faced the same problem. For no fault of hers, she was unable to bear children, not even a child. She did all she could, prayed, fasted and even at a point held the husband and said,

"Give me a child of my own".

However, it was clearly written that God himself was responsible, for he shut her womb. God had a plan. He needed to tell my generation and several generations to come that indeed, irrespective of the freedom we enjoy as part of our dominion over the earth, he has the power to shut and open, to give and take, to kill and to make alive.

What that means is that if you are facing a problem in life for no error or fault of yours or your environment, then look in God's direction. He may be responsible *but for a special purpose*! When you have no power or control over an issue, let it entirely to God and have faith that it shall be well again.

When Pharaoh of Egypt was so adamant to allow the children of Israel freedom from slavery in the land of Egypt, God's hand was in it. God was responsible because it was recorded that he (God) hardened *Pharaoh's heart* that he would not allow the children of Israel to go. Because God was responsible, not even the punishment of various measures meted on the Egyptians, could change the king's heart to allow them freedom. God did this for a purpose; to show forth his glory and power and majesty.

Is the problem in your life divine? Look around you and see if you've any fault, error, or attacks from wicked spirits. If not, check the handwriting of God around it. It is possible you are barren because God has other children that he wants you to care for; so that if he allows you children of your own, you could be carried away and not have time for the *other children*. Who knows, it is possible he created you to take care of others and not yours.

Similarly, having a child, wife or husband may be divine, so you could meet God at the right point.

The same manner, your car may refuse to start to divinely secure you out of an awaiting problem ahead. So many possibilities.

Now, from the Biblical point of view, God's faithfulness and mercy is indeed to those he chooses to have mercy on, but the question is that why having mercy on some and not on the others at the same time?

In fact, the most confusing aspect of it is that he sometimes fails completely to have mercy on those who seem to be His favourites, qualified to obtain mercy from Him. Example is when a pastor gets killed while preaching the gospel. He keeps silent when he ought not to, even to the "saint" or the "very elect". John the Baptist was beheaded. Maybe his assignment on earth was over, but they should have been another "humane" way in which to end a man's life. It got so bad in the prison that John had to send a message, out of frustration and discouragement, to Jesus and ask,

"Are you [*really*] the one who was to come, or should we expect someone else?" (Matthew 11:3).

This was because, things were really getting rough on the arrival of Christ and am very sure that John was expecting something pleasant at his coming. As if that was not enough, he got his head off him while he was still alive! Where was God all the while? He was there and he is still here. He was responsible so there was nothing anyone could do to prevent the situation.

Stephen was stoned to death for proclaiming God, through the name of Jesus. Jesus himself, for no sin or error of any kind, was killed on a cross; and out of frustration and pain, he cried to his father, and asked, "Oh father, why have you forsaken me"?

What about a situation where a burglar would narrowly escape from the hands of the law or even from an accident or something else and yet a faithful and morally behaved personality would not make it from such a situation? And the question remains "God, why? Some good people are not *successful* [please note that what constitutes a success, is largely subjective], but some known bad people are *successful*. Sometimes, the evil people seem to live longer on earth while the good and upright ones do not live as much. God may be responsible.

To be a true Christian or Muslim have some major challenges too. Many new converts may find it difficult to cope because the good promises told them by those who converted may not happen as expected. The truth, however, is that even some of the preachers still have their own peculiar challenges, sometimes unknown to the rest of the world.

Believers too would have to work hard to feed, pay their rents, school fees, and security of their lives and properties. They may still get involved in accidents. Burglars may still attack them. They will still die at the end of it all.

In fact, Christ told his disciples,

"In this world, you shall have tribulations but take heart, I have overcome the world" – John 16:33 NKJV.

What does that even mean? It means that Christianity does not fortify anyone against the happenings in our environment. However, the beauty of it is that its truth and knowledge help those who understand its principles to cope during difficult and perilous times.

To live is by faith (trusting in God for the hope not yet seen), to accept the fate that comes with living faithfully.

> *"These all died in faith, not having received the promises, but having seen them afar off, and were persuaded of them, and embraced them, and confessed that they were strangers and pilgrims on the earth…and others were tortured, not accepting deliverance; that they might obtain a better resurrection: And others had trial of cruel mocking and scourging's, yea, moreover of bonds and imprisonment: They were stoned, they were sawn asunder, were tempted, were slain with the sword: they wandered about in sheepskins and goatskins; being destitute, afflicted, tormented…they wandered in deserts, and in mountains, and in dens and caves of the earth….And these all, having obtained a good report through faith, received not the promise"* – Hebrew 11: 13, 35-39.

The promise of a new king, Jesus Christ that God promised our ancestors never came to them in their lifetime but later came thousands of years later. This is how God operates, ladies and gentlemen.

Pathetically, sometimes miracles will be happening to those who do not actually asked God for them, but it wouldn't just happen to those that have prayed ceaselessly for such miracles for years. For example, very poor people may have more children than they can care for. Meanwhile, someone somewhere who has all it takes to take care of a dozen children, may be struggling to conceive. It is because the parties involved are obeying the Universal Law on reproduction and as such, the reward and the reproach must have to follow accordingly.

A powerful man of God was involved in a ghastly motor accident, and he lost his life. While he laid in his casket, a dedicated women leader in his church, walked up to him and said, "Man of God, even you too could die in accident?"

She finished saying this in great tears, but the man never responded. She wept bitterly even more but the man of God never responded.

Now, are some things like his death in accident, the results of sins? First, I would say no but I would not say no in other circumstances. It is yes, if man is to blame but no, if God was at work. For example, if someone with 50 years' car driving experience should fall asleep while driving a car, disaster may be inevitable, his many years of experience notwithstanding. The years of experience will not help when control is lost.

As earlier pointed out, the reason everything around us happens the way they do is because everything in the universe is governed by Universal Laws. This allows equal treatment for everyone irrespective of religious affiliations. From the beginning of time, God gave man dominion and the will to make choices. This dominion and will is contained in the laws, which now put every man in a position such that whatever you do and whatever you get out of what you do, is now based on which of the laws you've obeyed and/or adopted in your way of life. In other words, since every law has conditions attached, it means that at any point in time any one of us meets the condition(s) stipulated for any of the laws, the law will take effect.

This is the reason why a teenager can get pregnant, and sinners get successful sometimes. The conditions for pregnancy and success respectively, have been met by the two situations mentioned above, so the law must take effect even if the persons involved are prepared or not, holy, or not holy, born again or not. The law must take effect; and God has no say. That is why He is silent.

"For there is no difference between the Jew and the Greek: for the same Lord over all is rich unto all that call upon him". Romans 10-12

In fact, the profit of this world is not for one person or for some group of people; it is for all of us.

"The profit of the earth is for all…" According to *Ecclesiastes 5 verse 9 (KJV).*

CHAPTER RECAPS

When some situations do not seem to give way to any solution being offered, think again; God may be the one responsible. If he is the one responsible, then pray for the grace to live with it. Somethings may change, others will remain till death bring everything to an end. No man can fight nature. No one can fight God. When He wants it, he will respond.

If a man does well from the start of his life and goofed at the very end, the Creator says he had lived all his life doing badly instead of good. If another man does the opposite, the Creator says he had done well. That is God. And truly, the end justifies the means.

Chapter Fifteen
THE WAY FORWARD

If there is anything that causes people to nag, fight, defraud, cheat, hate, disrespect, and pride, it is selfishness. Either one or both of the parties concerned are selfish. Everyone wants things their way. Often you hear some persons use the word "my" indiscriminately; know that selfishness is not far away.

Marriam Webster's Dictionary defined selfish as follows:

Concerned excessively or exclusively with oneself: seeking or concentrating on one's own advantage, pleasure, or well-being without regard for others; arising from concern with one's own welfare or advantage in disregard of others.

The results of selfishness are dangerous!

It may interest you to know once again that the problem of humankind is humankind. For sure, I know that if I choose not to steal from you and you do the same to me and to every other person on the face of the earth, it will mean that if I should keep an item in a point, I should meet it again when I want to! However, because everyone seeks himself or herself, in the process of serving ourselves, we overlook other people's feelings and live the virus lifestyle.

A virus is usually concerned with its replication at the expense of the host. It has some genetic materials solely concerned with its own replication; and that is why it is hard to remove it from wherever it attaches itself, both in plants and animals – they just keep multiplying!

Our experiences in life differ. Sometimes, the people we thought would never fail us ended up failing us completely. Many times, they failed to listen to our silent cries, or they totally refused to see through our feelings. At times, they keep the vineyard of other people's house and ignorantly leave theirs to weeds. Many times, they hear our cries, yet they refuse to listen. Many times, they could see clearly that our faces are reflections of crying hearts and minds, still, they refuse to observe. Many times, they just refuse to appreciate our efforts. Sometimes, all they care about is themselves and no one else. Many times, they show you no regard or respect as a son, daughter, pastor or even a spouse.

At such times, your voice goes low as you hold your breath in your hand, seeing your heaven collapse before you. The ones that ought to be your voice failed you, probably because of their selfishness.

When your voice goes low, the people that should speak for you, support you, encourage you and stand by you, become your sources of nightmares. In that regard, some parents have failed. Sisters have failed us. Brothers, uncles, and aunties have failed us. Even friends whom we open our hearts and secrets to …have failed us!

Even as I write this book under candlelight, sweating and trying to see how I could make the light brighter, my voice is going low.

The consequences of delayed actions that cause one's voice to go low is that tomorrow may be too late to help, appreciate and love. We are all working to make the world a better place, but if your behaviour today is not geared towards that, then you are the enemy that is making the environment uninhabitable. Therefore, if there is anything in your character that needs to be changed for good, please do it today and never tomorrow.

Periods of death for instance, is a period of sober reflection; whether you are the one about to die or someone you love is about to or has just died. A few characteristics of periods like these are crying and gnashing of teeth.

People cry over the death of someone for different reasons. Sometimes, some people cry because they can see clearly, that one day, it will be their turn to dance to the music of death too. Others cry because the dead people are their loved ones. Still, some cry because the deceased had failed them in one way or

When a Doctor Falls Ill

the other or they have failed the dead one in some way.

When I lost my cousin some years ago, I had different reasons to cry for his death. In fact, when the news of his death came to me, the first thing I remembered was the time we were fighting over a plate of food not too long before his death. I was the older one, therefore, when our food is served, traditionally, I, being the older, should take my share first before him. However, that day, he chose his own before me. Not that the food was not enough; it was, but because I felt the "due process" was not followed, I objected and reacted, but he insisted he was right.

The next thing that happened was… too bad and unnecessary! I kicked his plate of food off his hand. The impact of the kick was so much that the plate almost penetrated the ceiling boards of the living room.

At the end of it all, I had to share my plate of food with him. So, immediately I heard the news of his death, my mind took me back to this very scene and I screamed…

"Lord, I should have left the food for him!

…but it was too late to do that; too late to show him how much I loved him and how much I wished him well, even though we fought over mundane things. I was too selfish because I wanted it my way.

The second thing that made me cry was the fact that death is inevitable. It amazes me a lot how an active, strong, and nimble human being could become so weak and completely inactive! We played rigorous football and other games together, but there he was in his grave, allowing tons of earth on him and yet, he never reacted. He was buried; and that was when I accepted that indeed, he had died.

And my voice went low.

My voice went low because I forgot that man shall not live by bread alone. My voice went low because I thought he might "cheat" me another day. My voice went low because I was ignorant of tomorrow, of what truly matters.

"Man shall not live by bread alone" – Matthew 4:4.

My voice went low because I never thought death could come at such an early age and time. My voice went low because, I forgot that by due process, it was not even fit for purpose except by the grace of God.

If you've the opportunity to turn the pillars of your community and friends around, you need not wait for tomorrow. If you've the means to actualize someone's dream, you need not wait for tomorrow and keep his or her voice low anymore. If you can change the world and make it a better place, you need not wait until tomorrow. Christ gave His all. He gave his life so that you and I will no longer talk in low voices, crying and sobering. He gave his life so that we can have access to the throne anytime without going to Jerusalem or the mountains. He gave His life for us to live. He offered us a loud voice such that we were like them that dream when we count our blessings.

He did all these, so that when a doctor falls ill, the doctor of doctors can step into the boat.

David observed this and he sang a song saying:

When the LORD turned again the captivity of Zion, we were like them that dream. Psalms 126:1

The only time you have got to love and appreciate your children, your spouse, the church, and everyone around you is not when death comes, but as life remains. Moses knew this fact also and he cried unto God in prayer saying:

"Teach us oh LORD to number our days, that we may apply our hearts unto wisdom." - Psalms 90:12.

Look beside you, inside of you and anywhere he/she can be found; a friend is always by your side when your voice goes low. He has, He is, and He is to come. He is a friend that never fails. He cries when you cry. He loves you more than you know. When everyone else departs from you, he is there by your side. Friends, parents, spouse may fail you, but he is always there any day. He is the one who told the harlot, did any man cast a stone on thee or condemn thee? Then the harlot replied:

"No man, Lord. And Jesus said unto her, neither do I condemn thee: go, and sin no more." John 8:11.

God does not condemn anyone who has finally made it to the world. You now have the chance that others have, whether your parents were married or not. So, rise to it. The truth is that he uses people like you and me to meet people's needs. Should you know that you are a pillar that can make things happen in someone's life, do not wait until tomorrow comes. For God to turn the captivity of Zion around he used men; and for the book of Psalms to be written, David and Moses, had to sing songs.

In addition, anytime you face a particular problem in your life that does not seem to give way to your prayers and fasting, know that it is like *when a doctor falls ill*, only one man can help him; and that is our Heavenly Father. However, he does this at his own appointed time. Treat your problems, conditions and life challenges the way the three Hebrew young men treated their situations when they were face to face with the wrath of King Nebuchadnezzar and death.

"We know that our Lord can deliver us from your hands oh king…. but peradventure he chose not to deliver us, we would not still bow down to your golden image" Daniel 3:17-28.

To me, that should be the summary of Christianity and living a life to the fullest.

What is the way forward you may be asking? The answer is right there in one of the books of the Prophets.

"…seek the peace of the city where I have caused you to be carried away captives and pray unto the LORD for it: for in the peace thereof shall you've peace." Jeremiah 29: 7.

If you choose to pray for the peace of Nigeria, you may have a peaceful life. If you choose to be good to the people around you, your life will be good. The ball is now in the court of humanity to make his dwelling place a haven.

For those who feel they have overcome all the hurdles of life and have made it in all ramifications, there is a way forward still: Seeking Significance.

Begin to seek significance.

As obtainable all over the world during funerals, it is often said that *"from dust we all came, and to dust we shall all return"*, that statement is simply a complete definition of the uselessness of human bodies at death. The essence of burial is to put the dead body away from disturbing normal living. It is a complete definition of worthlessness! The only useful part of a dead person is what he or she had done while alive. Those things are the significance you should start seeking immediately.

Seek Significance!

CHAPTER RECAPS

People whose lives have tints of significance are the gods. The gods are not some invisible forces anywhere; rather they are the people with significance. You are the gods!

The gods speaks even when they are dead. When they are alive, they exhibit power, authority, and make things happen. Sometimes, they do not need to announce their presence, others do that for them. When they are eventually dead, they still speak. They speak through books, songs, and legacies.

The only ways the dead can speak to you is through reading books written by them, listening to songs by them or by benefiting from legacies left by them. In other words, if you have not authored a book, nor sung a song or other related medias, nor left a legacy in the sand of time, when you die you will never be heard again.

Every man has three tools to use to become significant: books, multimedia, & legacies. One man

When a Doctor Falls Ill

can exhibit the three or two or even one if he so wishes. You can be the man you want to be.

Is somebody seeking significance already? Please begin today. Tomorrow may never come.

Arise and work, for good!

Chapter Sixteen
STRATEGISE WITH PARTNERSHIP

In 2020, shortly before Corona Virus became a pandemic, I ran into a man in London while checking into a hotel. He was in an argument with the hotel's receptionist, and I was the next in line to check in, so I listened. He wanted something from the hotel, I think smoking in his room without the need to come out to the smoking area outside the hotel building. Unfortunately, the UK law on smoking indoors or in a car with children changed from around 2015. He argued this fact in vain.

Then he dropped a bombshell: "I don't follow rules," he exclaimed.

When I checked his hand, he was holding a car key. My immediate thought was that, if he drove to the hotel, he would have followed countless number of rules. Driving is a serious exercise, and it is not surprising that a license is required to drive on public roads in most countries of the world, except in places with no stable government.

So far in this book, I have been able to show that there are rules and regulations to every facet of our lives. There are terms and conditions to every offer, even offers that are "free". I can guarantee you that nothing is absolutely free.

Now, the other part of that discussion is the strategy required to get things done within the rules and regulations, within the terms and conditions.

One of the key elements of your strategy is partnership.

I have received random messages from relatives and friends, asking for financial support for their "business ideas", or even for an existing business. One of the first things that comes to my mind each time I receive these kinds of requests is that the people asking for money do not know how to make money at all. Information is power, and it is very important to know how to become rich and stay rich. It is important to know how to finance your ideas.

Here is a fact you must know: every wealthy human being wants their wealth to keep growing. Anything that would stagnate them or reduce their wealth, is a threat! Read that again. If you want to just "take" out of their wealth, you are a threat to them!

So, when you ask them to "give" you money for "your" business, you are threatening them. You want your business to grow, against theirs. You want to grow your money to their detriment.

It does not work that way.

You should ask for partnership rather than asking them for free money (it is a threat to their wealth). As you want to grow, show how their money (the one you are asking them to give you) will grow through your business.

There are many benefits of partnership, and chief among them is the increased leverage you get when you find a partner with the same vision as yours. It is also easier to set up, compared to a limited liability company.

Partnering with someone means the burden of the business is shared, as well as the profit. Someone could provide the funds; another could run the business. The percentage of the partnership can easily be agreed. New partners can be welcomed into the fold easily too. The overall benefit is that there is a better chance of making better decisions (two good heads are better than one, right?). Oh yes.

Finally, the business can go on if one of the partners dies, and with trust, the shares of the deceased can be transferred to loved ones or sold to a new person. Do not do it alone, seek partnership today!

Chapter Seventeen
TAKE THE RISK

At all times, breaking a barrier or limitation requires some level of force or risks. Nothing gets done on its own: someone had to do something. For every action, there is an opposite reaction, so it is possible you could fail if you take some risks. For you to get a better chance of succeeding, you must take risks that are predictable, so you can prepare a counter-offensive.

The title of this chapter is a full book title by Dr Ben Carson and Gregg Lewis. In the book, they talked about learning to identify, choose, and live with acceptable risks. Ben Carson became popular after he led a team of neurosurgeons to operate and separate conjoined twins in September 1987. The operation was the first of its kind, and it was a huge risk that could end his medical career or project him to the entire world as one of the most gifted neurosurgeons in the world. He is a Black man.

When a Doctor Falls Ill

He had worked out Four Simple Questions to Help Assess Any Risk:

What is the worst thing that can happen if you take this risk?

What is the best thing that could happen if you take the risk?

What is the worst thing that could happen if you DON'T take this risk?

What is the best thing that could happen if you DON'T take the risk?

We are confronted with tough situations that require tough decisions at times and I don't see any better feeling than having to finally convince yourself on the next step to take. Ben Carson's Four Questions came in handy and optimally useful in every of such decisions.

Does it mean every time I applied this Questions, I get all my decisions correct and successful. Hell no! It never worked out successfully all the time for Ben Carson himself. What it does to you personally, however, is useful, engaging, and peaceful to the mind to be termed "unsuccessful". If it didn't work out as planned, then it didn't work out as planned.

The thing is, at some points in your life, you must take a risk to breakthrough. I have tried doing all kinds of businesses, and I have failed in many of them too, but looking back, if have a chance to make those decisions again, I will. However, with the lessons learnt, there is a chance to make a better decision.

Once I met someone on social media who, for some reason, decided to engage me privately. He told me his ideas and requested my input. Normally, I would have seen the engagement as an attempt to defraud me. Scammers can be very convincing! I reluctantly shared my thoughts with him, based on what he shared with me.

He had sent me his full business plan, and I was really caught up with it. I made my recommendations and sent them back to him. The part that got me scared was that he needed money to execute this business. He showed me the list of friends and family members that had contributed to this idea, and how much he had held in the bank towards this. He still needed One Million Naira more.

I was terrified by this request.

I have learnt that doing business is a risk. I also know that investing in a small business as an entrepreneur, is even a higher risk. *"For me to put a penny to this business, I would have to travel to Lagos from London, to see things for myself first"*, I had typed in an email. But I could not send the email because embarking on this check will cost me more than a million. It could even cost me my life!

I started applying Ben Carson's Four Simple Questions to this business "opportunity."

What is the worst thing that can happen if you take this risk? I asked myself.

Answer|: I will lose my One Million Naira, and I will also lose trust in humanity a bit.

What is the best thing that could happen if you take the risk?

I would have helped a young entrepreneur execute a great business idea and may even recover my One Million Naira and more. A new partnership or relationship could emerge from this.

What is the worst thing that could happen if you DON'T take this risk?

Well, for me, I wouldn't have the chance to be part of this business adventure, but I will be thinking about this for the rest of my life, asking myself if I should have invested or not.

What is the best thing that could happen if you DON'T take the risk?

I will simply keep my One Million Naira and move on with my life, no questions!

When a Doctor Falls Ill

At this point in my life, one million Naira was not a big deal. However, it was a huge deal to the young entrepreneur I had not met.

I took the risk.

The first phase of the business was to run for six months, so, I did not hear much from him apart from his occasional social media posts, highlighting his products and deliveries to clients. It looked good.

On the 7th month, I had received Four Million Naira alert and then a message that simply sys, "Thank you for believing in me and my family. We did it big." I was indeed happy. This went down well.

On another occasion, it did not! Because I ignored Ben Carson's questions. A cousin had messaged me on Facebook, and we started chatting. He had told me how he lost his job and then returned to the village, being unable to secure another job in Lagos.

I felt sorry for him.

I once felt sorry for him in the past too. He had just finished a National Diploma, no job, and no money to proceed for a Higher National Diploma. He had messaged me on Facebook just to say hi. As usual, I asked how he was doing, and he narrated his situation. I felt it was better if he got a job first. So, I called a friend in Abuja, and we arranged for him to get a temporal employment. The reason I wanted to pull him out of the village is that opportunities available to him in the village are limited, almost non-existent. In fact, there was a limited mobile network in the village then, and that would have limited his chances even more.

I asked for his account details, and I was shocked that he had none! He sent his father's bank account details, and I sent some money that could get him to Abuja and for upkeep for a few days. Soon, he told me that an old friend had called him to suggest they go for their HND. The friend's dad is rich, and he volunteered to pay his fees.

It was good news. He left for the school soon after.

So, when he told me about the job he lost, I contacted a few friends who were willing to invest in creating the kind of business his former employer was doing. He had over 3 years' experience, according to him.

I did not analyse the risks in this venture. And once he received the start-up fund, he stopped communicating, and soon disappeared from the network. It was a loss for me, and I had to repay my friends the money they invested in the business.

Over the years, I have learnt lessons when dealing business deals. Number one of it is that, having business deals with relatives or church/mosque members does not reduce the risks in the business. In fact, it doubles the risk involved. Never ever deal a business deal without adequate checks and balances.

Do not forget to pen down your agreement. Even with your friends, state the terms and conditions of all your deals.

Should you take the risks? Oh yes. Take calculated risks, and there would be a 50 to 70% chance of getting it right. That is the way to go!

Chapter Eighteen
BE USEFUL

It may interest you to know that I postponed the publication date of this book because of this chapter. Recently, I have seen friends, family members and others complaining about their "unhelpful" relatives such as brothers, sisters, and uncles. I would hear or read comments like, "he has money, but refused to help me".

If you are one of those with "unhelpful" relatives, it is time to check and ask yourself this question: are you useful to them?

Are you useful to them?

This question must be answered with honesty. I have half-brothers that could have been able to do certain things in my absence, but I found myself sending other people most of the times. Other people seem to deliver authentic result that they do, so I prefer sending people I do not know, instead of sending them. The reason is simple: they just cannot deliver results. That does not mean they are not useful, but they would have made me and themselves better if they could understand me and do more. I do send them on errands, but I do so within the limit they know. I wish they knew more, improved their versatility (or usefulness).

Some people have valid reasons to avoid their relatives when it comes to financial investment. I had invested millions of Nigerian Naira in people's businesses because the businesses have potentials. I have no idea how those people got their skills; all I know is that they have something that can grow. Therefore, it is easy for them to get investors into their business.

The question again is this: are you useful?

You want your uncle to give you a million Naira for "your own" business just like that? No, it does not work like that. He worked for his money, and he wants the money to grow. To get a million Naira out of his pocket, you must come with ideas, potential ideas that can grow yourself and his money without him losing out his money to you.

A few months ago, I wanted to buy a piece of land for an estate in Nigeria, but I was far from home. I was in London. My lawyer had written the deeds, and I needed it printed out in Nigeria. I could not send my half-brothers from my mother's side, because they do not know how to get it done. It was a paid service to receive the documents, print them and submit it to the local council securely, but they had no idea what to do. I had to hire someone else! Yes, they were my brothers; they could have made some money doing just this, but they were not useful in this regard. They do not know how to use technology; they do not know anything about confidentiality either.

Someone may say: why don't you train them to know how to do all that? Well, ask who trained me first.

You see, you must find a way to place yourself in a position of value. These brothers and sisters do receive surprise money from me – with no assignment attached. They received money for Christmas, they received above their school fees value. Those little tips are for self-development. The "free" monies are not for new phones.

Add value to yourself. Be useful. Position yourself in a place where you are needed. That is your job to do. If you are not getting the help you need, it is time to re-examine your usefulness too. It may be the reason you are not breaking through yet. Be useful.

Thank you for your time. This edition had limited editorial team, so please pardon me for any error or omission. For comments and other enquiries, email dr.ahiaba@gmail.com

Printed in Great Britain
by Amazon